Plenty
for
Everyone

Corrie ten Boom

Fort Washington, PA 19034

Published by CLC Publications

U.S.A.
P.O. Box 1449, Fort Washington, PA 19034

GREAT BRITAIN
51 The Dean, Alresford, Hants. SO24 9BJ

AUSTRALIA
P.O. Box 2299, Strathpine, QLD 4500

NEW ZEALAND
10 MacArthur Street, Feilding

ISBN (13): 978-0-87508-983-6

Contents

Foreword

Glancing superficially at the contents of this little book, one gains the impression that it is a diverting hodge-podge of vivid personal experiences interspersed with sermonettes. Yet, even skipping through, the reader can scarcely fail to be arrested. In a breath-taking way a sentence, a quotation, an incident, flashes out with inescapable challenge. "Is there anything for which you cannot pray?" is a simple but searching question which confronts the reader unexpectedly at the end of a rather amusing experience of Corrie ten Boom's when praying in an airplane. As is her custom she was asking God's help and blessing on every aspect of the journey—until she came to the three watches she was planning to smuggle into Holland. Her inability to pray for success in that enterprise convinced her that she must declare them after all! What she could not pray for she should not try to do.

As we read we discover that for all her agonizing experiences at the hands of the Nazis, and for all her molding in the hands of God, she is still a very human woman, subject to like passions as we ourselves. There are times when the author feels sorry for herself, irritated with others and is ready to take the easy way out from a life of continual travel. Some may be tempted to wonder why such a person sees such spectacular conversions as the result of simple preaching. But there is a sharp, two-edged sword which works effectively in her before it flashes out at us. Herein lies the secret of the power of her ministry.

This little book deserves more than a superficial reading. In it is the unconscious revelation of God's mighty working in the soul of one who walks in sincerity before Him.

Those who are prepared to do the same can but only profit by what Corrie ten Boom has written in this her sixth book.

Phyllis Thompson
London, 1967

One

Plenty for Everyone

Go ye . . . (Matt. 28:19)

When the disciples were passing out the food to the five thousand, they must have rejoiced in their hearts, seeing the miracle-plenty for everyone. So when a Christian receives the happy Biblical messages, straight from the hands of Jesus, he too will experience—plenty for everyone.

In this book I shall be describing some of the experiences which have been mine as a bearer of the gospel in different countries. This means that I must be constantly "on the go," living out of a suitcase; but the joy of doing such work for the Lord is tremendous, no matter where He may send me.

The stories you will read are true and the quotations taken from clippings in my notebook: a portable library containing those things which I have heard, and read, and written down for use in the ministry of the gospel. Yet this book, into which these stories have been woven, is not a diary; neither is it meant to be a handbook for soul-winners.

My personal contact with people is often too brief. Although I like to do more thorough work and speak at least six times to the same audience, I am often permitted to speak only once to the same group of people. Then I grumble and feel unhappy. Nevertheless I see how the Lord blesses these "once only" meetings. Then I must thank Him and repent of my grumbling.

I have no other choice; I must obey. I am so rich. I have a book, the Bible: what a book! It is full of rich promises, blessings, realities—full of our Savior Himself, Jesus Christ. I have the privilege to share this good news of plenty almost every day with people in different parts of the world. My experience will give you a glimpse of what a joy it is to spread the gospel. Not many are called to the same kind of traveling service. Only after my fifty-fourth year did God ordain for me to become a "tramp for the Lord." Before that time I lived for more than fifty years in the same house in Haarlem, Holland.

But it is not such a great difference to speak to people in your homeland as anywhere else in the world. Every Christian is called to be on duty twenty-four hours every day in "the King's business." Your office, your school, your kitchen, your drawing-room, your factory, all are a mission field. Jesus still says, "Give the hungry to eat."

Once when I was at Lee Abbey, a conference center in England, I heard someone say, "Is not Corrie ten Boom wonderful?"

Then I knew there was something wrong. I had to humble myself. I had looked in the opposite direction. When we look unto Jesus He makes us a mirror of His joy. The Holy Spirit glorifies Jesus; and when we are Spirit-filled He uses our lips to praise Jesus and not ourselves. Then people will say, "Is not Jesus wonderful?"

A LEGEND

As my Father hath sent me, even so send I you. (John 20:21)

Dr. Billy Graham has said, "We Christians are debtors. We owe the world the gospel." Yes, we can do nothing more important than share the good news of Jesus. It is our{/nly response to the Lord in thankfulness for our plentiful salvation. I once read a legend about Christ's return to heaven, when He had finished His work in this world. As He arrived at the shore of heaven the angels ran to meet Him, eagerly questioning Him about His work on earth among men.

"Did you complete your work of redemption?"

"Yes, it is finished."

"Who will make it known?"

"I have told Peter, John, Philip and all who are my disciples."

"And what if they fail?"

"I have no other plan, and they will not fail."

How is it that Jesus can trust to our care the important task of taking the gospel to the lost all over the world? The grand answer is that He has given us all that is necessary for the task. First, the Holy Spirit is there to give us power. In Acts 1:8 (Amp.) we read, "But you shall receive power—ability, efficiency and might—when the Holy Spirit has come upon you." Following this promise is the order to march, "And you shall be My witnesses in Jerusalem and all Judea and Samaria and to the ends—the very bounds—of the earth."

Second, He has given us the boundless resources of the Bible, a book of good news—and plenty of it! It gives the answers to all the problems of mankind. Every one of God's promises is backed by the golden reserves of the bank of heaven, with God watching over His word to perform it. If we stand before the "plenty" of God's great riches, our amazement is more at the grace of God which enables us to be channels of all His love and goodness. No wonder Paul exclaimed, "Unto me, who am less than the least of all saints, is this grace given, that I should preach among the Gentiles the unsearchable riches of Christ" (Eph. 3:8). Whichever way Paul turned, as Dr. J. H. Jowett pointed out, the avenues and turnings are lined with God's shining grace, unsuspected and beyond description.

And so I set out. He said, "Go ye . . ." He has given me His plenty and provided His mighty power with which to share this plenty to feed the world's multitudes. Come with me and see some of the great things that the Lord has done.

Two

Paratroopers

Servants, be obedient to them that are your masters. (Eph. 6:5)

A paratroop instructor said that there are four commands which he gives his parachutists:

> First: Attention!
> Second: Stand in the door!
> Third: Lookup !
> Fourth: Follow me!

Then the men have to jump.

Jesus is preparing men and women for the new heaven and the new earth and has given His co-workers the same orders as the parachutists receive. It is not our task to give God His instructions: we must report for duty.

FIRST: ATTENTION

No man cometh unto the Father, but by me. (John 14:6)

Some people do not believe that there are souls to be saved for eternity. They think, rather, that everyone will be saved as a matter of course. They need to hear the bad news before the glad news has any value.

During the last war friends often warned me of the danger of working in the underground movement to save the Jewish people in Holland and told of the cruel treatment which would befall me if I should be caught and sent to a concentration camp. To such warnings I always replied that these stories of such atrocities could not be true, that they must surely be anti-German propaganda; and so I turned a deaf ear to them. But did my deaf ear help me when I was in Ravensbruck and saw my sister and thousands of other people perish at the hands of the Nazis? It did not help me at all. And neither will it help a person, when he is in hell, to have disbelieved in the existence of hell.

If we love our fellow men, we must tell them of the danger of a lost eternity, of Jesus who came and lived among men to teach and warn them, and of His death on the cross to save them from the agonizing darkness in an eternity shut off from God. For He, and only He, is "the way, the truth, and the life"; as His Word also teaches:

> Whosoever believeth in him [Jesus] should not perish, but have everlasting life. (John 3:16)
> God has given men eternal life and this real life is to be found only in his Son. (1 John 5:11, Phillips)
> The man who believes in the Son has eternal life. The man who refuses to believe in the Son will not see life; he lives under the anger of God. (John 3:36, Phillips)

I have seen people ready to go wherever they were sent in order to take a message of a godless philosophy all over the world. They have surrendered their bodies, souls, minds, family lives, money, time and in fact their all for the sake of their convictions.

We Christians are called to bring to a hungry world the bread of life: the message of salvation, love, eternal life, riches immeasurable and a peace that passes all understanding—God's plenty. But how can the world believe this message if they do not hear it, and how can they hear it if we do not tell them? It must be a case of: ATTENTION!

Could a mariner sit idle when he heard the drowning cry?
Could a doctor sit in comfort knowing that his patient die?
Could a fireman watch men perish and not give a helping
   hand?
Can you sit at ease in Zion with a world around condemned?

SECOND: STAND IN THE DOOR!

Go ye therefore, and teach all nations. (Matt. 28:19)

In my travels throughout the world, I have often visited mission fields; and what a joy it has been to be used by God for the strengthening of missionaries. But there are far more women than men in this work for the Lord; and I think there must have been some young men who, when surrendering their lives to Jesus Christ, prayed, "Here I am, Lord, but do send my sister."

Peter said, "No, my Lord," but had to learn that he could not say "No" if he said 'my Lord," nor "my Lord" if he said "No." "Stand in the door" means that we must be obedient and go where God tells us, whether it be a call to the mission field or a call to work for Him at home. He can use us only when we are in the place where He wants us to be. We dare not hoard the gospel secret but must herald forth His story to all.

THIRD: LOOK UP!

*But we all, with unveiled face reflecting as a mirror the glory of
the Lord, are transformed into the same image from glory to glory.*
(2 Cor. 3:18, R.V.)

When we look at ourselves we are sure that we are unable to be used by the Lord; but when we look to Jesus, we
become His mirrors. It is true that, of itself, a mirror does
not do much; but when it is hung or placed in the right
position, it does its job properly. It is very important, therefore, that we should be in the right position. And that position, for a Christian, is "looking unto Jesus the author and
finisher of our faith" (Heb. 12:2), for we have no light of
ourselves.

Unfortunately there are times in our lives when we experience a different truth: "Mine iniquities have taken hold
upon me [hindered me], that I am not able to look up" (Ps.
40:12). On these occasions it is very necessary for us to bring
our sins in repentance to the Lord Jesus and restore our vision of Calvary.

I have a small dictaphone, and when it breaks down I
do not make any attempt to repair it but return it instead
to the manufacturer, who restores it to its former efficiency.
In the same way, when my faith breaks down, I send it
back to the "Manufacturer," Jesus, for repair because when
He corrects the fault, it will most assuredly work properly
again. He is the Author and Finisher, the Manufacturer of
our faith.

Yes, let us always be in the right position, so that we can
be good mirrors for the Lord no matter what the circumstances may be.

I recall an occasion when I suffered a slight accident in my home town. The policeman who helped me pulled out his little notebook to record what had happened (for in Holland when something occurs in which the police are involved, it is always necessary for them to make a report).

"What is your name?"

"Corrie ten Boom."

He looked surprised and questioned me further, "Are you a member of the family of that name whom we arrested about ten years ago?"

"That is right."

During the war the good Dutch policeman had been in the service of the Gestapo, remaining there for the express purpose of helping the political prisoners. This man had been on duty the day that my family was arrested.

"I'll never forget that night in the police station," he said. "The atmosphere was more of victory than of horror at the thought of dying in prison or a concentration camp. I often tell the story of how your father, who so shortly afterwards was to die in prison, opened his Bible and read Psalm 91."

Even after ten years that policeman still remembered which psalm Father had read, the psalm which begins:

He that dwelleth in the secret place of the most High shall abide under the shadow of the Almighty.

When I arrive in heaven and see my father again, I shall ask him, "Do you remember that night in the police station in Haarlem?"

I think he will answer, "Yes! That was the last time we were all together."

"Do you remember the policeman who was on duty?"

It is more than possible that he will reply, "No; I don't remember," for Father was always a very relaxed person. He would never have thought to himself, *Now, I must do or say something which will be a blessing to this policeman.* It was simply that his life and eyes were turned towards Jesus. So on that terrible evening, he was made a mirror of God's light. As in the poem I once jotted down:

> *When we enter the beautiful city,*
> *And the saved all around us appear,*
> *We'll hear from several people,*
> *"It was you that invited me here."*

We will ask in amazement, "Did I invite you to heaven?" Then we will learn that it was during the time we were looking unto Jesus, mirroring His joy. We are not suns to burn others with our "self-goodness," just moons to reflect His dear light.

FOURTH: FOLLOW ME!

Bear the cross; wear the crown.
(An embroidered motto in a farm in India.)

Whosoever will come after me, let him deny himself,
and take up his cross, and follow me. (Mark 8:34)

Denying ourselves, taking up our crosses and following Jesus is not like jumping from an airplane towards earth with parachutes on our backs. It means being safe in the hands of Jesus, yoke-fellows with Him—His joy in us, and our joy fulfilled. Paratroopers for Jesus must trust Him. Our commission is to bring the gospel of plenty to the whole world, and Jesus has promised us His Holy Spirit and His power to do the work (Acts 1:8).

When we trust ourselves we are doing the wrong thing. We can fall into the error of spiritual pride on the one hand, or discouragement on the other. We are really strong when we are weak; weak when we are strong. A branch cannot bring forth fruit of itself, but however strong or weak it may be, it will bring forth much fruit if it is connected to the vine. When it is connected, the branch is given the nature of the vine. So following on in the footsteps of Jesus, taking the steps (yes, and the jumps into the unknown) we can become the paratroopers. We can storm the enemy's territory and win souls for Jesus—but only if we obey. "Follow Me . . ."; then His promise takes effect: "I will make you fishers of men."

Three

Prisoners

*God has chosen what the world calls weak to shame the strong.
He has chosen things of little strength and small repute . . . to
explode the pretensions of the things that are—that no man may
boast in the presence of God.* (1 Cor. 1:27–29, Phillips)

In a New Zealand prison I once spoke about the great commission which the Lord has given us: "As my Father hath
sent me, even so send I you" (John 20:21).

This is a commission for every Christian wherever he
may be, even in a prison.

Why did God send Jesus? To seek what was lost. Why
did Jesus send us? To seek what is lost. Jesus said that we are
lights in the world, the salt of the earth! All the requirements
necessary for being an ambassador for Christ are contained
in the Word of God. Acts 1:8 records the commission and
the provision. Because we receive power after the Holy Spirit
has come upon us, we can become witnesses to Jesus Christ
in Jerusalem, in Samaria and in Judea, and to the uttermost
parts of the earth.

After my talk in the prison, one of the Christians thanked
me with well-chosen words. Prisoners' morale is helped by
these polite "rules" of etiquette, for they suffer much from

inferiority and failure. Even to make a speech, like an official "thank you," does much toward restoring their self-respect.

When the man had finished his little speech, he turned to his fellow prisoners and said, "Fellows, this morning I read my Bible and found stories about three murderers used by God! Their names were Moses, David and Paul: how God used them! There is hope for you and me, fellows, when we see what God can do with 100% surrendered sinners!"

Sometimes I hear the best sermons from the mouths of prisoners. Many of these hard cases baffle Christian workers and elude our efforts of help: God is never baffled.

When Francis of Assisi was asked, late in life, how it was he had accomplished so much for God, his answer was in this way:

> This must be why the Lord has blessed my efforts. He looked down from heaven and must have said, "Where can I find the weakest, the smallest, the meanest man on the face of the earth?" Then He saw me and said, "Now I have found him. I will work through him, for he will not be proud of it nor take My honor away from Myself. He will realize that I am using him because of his littleness and insignificance."

Prison Darkness and Light

What a wonderful Savior is Jesus, my Lord!
For the Son of man is come to seek and to save
that which was lost. (Luke 19:10)

In Manila I was given the opportunity of speaking in a huge state prison called Montinlupa. As I was known as a prison speaker in many places throughout the world, a public address system had been installed which enabled me to reach about seven thousand criminals in all the buildings and cells.

The beginning was a little alarming; to reach my destination inside the prison, I had to go through two doors bearing the sign: SECURITY LIMIT. I understood that in some way I was taking my life into my own hands by going through them: I had been told that just the week before fifty-seven prisoners had been murdered by their fellow prisoners.

Very few guards went with us; but a young woman, Mrs. Olga Robertson, who every Saturday went to teach a prisoners' Bible class, accompanied me. This lady had accomplished a remarkable work. As soon as a prisoner accepted the Lord as his Savior, she arranged for him to have a correspondence course in Bible study. Some of them she even had trained as leaders to form other groups of Bible students. As more and more leaders became qualified to take charge of a group, they requested to be transferred to other parts of the prison where they could start new Bible classes. There existed forty of these studies at the time of my visit.

There was plenty of time for Bible study as these prisoners had no regular work to do as in other prisons (To arrange work for so many is not easy). Mrs. Robertson was able to speak to them only once a week and gave others instruction by means of a correspondence course. When a prisoner had completed his course, he was given a certificate. This lady is a living example of God's miraculous work in this dark, dark prison.

There were about four hundred prisoners in the square where the microphone was placed. On the towers in each corner of the square stood guards, armed with machine-guns, keeping an especially watchful eye on those with bright orange uniforms: I learned later that these were the incorrigibles. I searched my heart to see if there was any fear. Indeed I did find tension, wondering what would happen among such criminals.

And then—what a surprise was waiting for me! The moment I entered, a band of about ninety prisoners began to play the chorus,

> There is power, power, wonder-working power,
> In the precious blood of the Lamb.

The last fraction of apprehension left my heart, and I experienced one of those moments when my cup runs over with joy. The bandmaster handed me a card on which, in bright colors, had been painted a welcome for me by one of the artists among the prisoners. Then in broken English he gave an official speech on behalf of all the men.

A wonderful joy entered me as I spoke into that microphone, for I knew that I was reaching many people who had never before heard the gospel. In my hands I held the Book, the Bible, containing the many promises and answers to the problems in the hearts of these, and of all, men. Because of the message in this Book, I could tell them that every soul is precious in God's sight.

I had been told that in the death cells fifty men were awaiting execution in the electric chair. So to them, after I had finished my talk, I gave an extra message:

I know a little bit how you feel; for once I was in solitary confinement for four months, never sure whether anyone stopping outside my door had come to kill me or not. I did not know that my release would come just one week previous to the execution of all women of my age in that camp. So you see, fellows, I have looked death in the eyes more than once; yet it was in those moments that I realized how rich I was.

I have in my hand the Bible. In this book you can read how you can go to heaven after death and how God, in so loving the world, sent His only Son, Jesus, to earth to solve our sin and death problems, so that everyone who believes in Him will not perish but have everlasting life. Believing in Him, I could say in the moment when I had to face death, "Thanks be to God who giveth us the victory through our Lord Jesus Christ." In the words of a hymn writer:

> *On Christ, the solid rock, I stand,*
> *All other ground is sinking sand.*

And this is for you too because Jesus died for the sins of the whole world and now lives as our Advocate with the Father. You have only to bring Him all your sins and then to receive Him as your Savior. He will make you happy for He gives you a new heart. Your souls are very precious in His sight.

As I went back to the door, someone put a small piece of paper into my hand. I waited until we had left the prison and then read: "I am in the cell. I have heard your message. You have helped me very much. Please send us someone to tell us more about Jesus."

The second afternoon I challenged the men to make a

decision: "You are confronted with the living Jesus, and then there is always an answer to give. If you say 'yes' it can make you very, very rich. If you say 'no' then you are more in the power of the evil one than before."

That night the prisoners killed seven of their fellows. I trembled when I heard, realizing that my words had had a more true application than I first thought. The guards told us that permission could not be granted for us to enter the next day as it was too dangerous. So we prayed that God would open the prison doors instead; and He did. We were told we could enter but only at our own risk.

The men were nervous but ready to listen that afternoon while I spoke on the text: "The wages of sin is death; but the gift of God is eternal life. . . ." (Rom. 6:23) While I was trying to show them the terrible and dangerous consequence of choosing the evil one instead of Jesus, I heard the sound of footsteps behind me, as the noise of chains being dragged over the gravel echoed. It was the murderers being taken to the questioning room with chained hands and feet.

I am not always fortunate enough to be permitted to speak three times in a prison as I was allowed to in Montinlupa, and I would like to ask your prayer that whenever I come to prisons the authorities will give me permission to speak several times to the men and women who have gone astray. For these also Jesus died—Jesus, who said, "As my Father hath sent me, even so send I you . . . To seek those who are lost."

Often I do not hear what happens afterwards; but in this case I kept in contact with Mrs. Robertson, who wrote to tell me about one of the men in the death cell. Later this man was visited by a Roman Catholic priest who had been sent to tell him that he was to die next day in the electric chair. This priest asked, "Will you make confessions of sins to me?"

"No," the man replied, "that is not necessary. I have brought all my sins to the Lord Jesus and He has cleansed me with His blood. He has cast them into the depths of the sea, and if I understood rightly, there is a sign which says, 'NO FISHING ALLOWED.'"

Twenty minutes before the hour fixed for his execution, the authorities telephoned to say he had been reprieved; a month later he was set free. I sometimes think that life is far more interesting than the most thrilling novel!

> *Got any rivers you think are uncrossable?*
> *Got any mountains you can't tunnel through?*
> *God specializes in things thought impossible,*
> *He can do just what none other can do.*

YES OR NO?

> *This child is set for the fall and rising again of many. . . .*
> (Luke 2:34)

> *What will you do with Jesus?*
> *Neutral you cannot be . . .*

We cannot be used to win souls, or to be open channels of blessing, if there is an unforgiving spirit or bitterness or resentment in our hearts. For love is the most important factor in soul-winning. It is when we depend upon God's love that we can experience miracles.

During the war there were two of my own countrymen associated with the arrests of my family. Their hardness and cruelty far outweighed that of anyone else who had to do with our detention. It was a horrible experience for our old father to be sent to prison with all his children, three daughters and a son, to say nothing of a grandson and about forty friends. But the callousness of these two guards, plus the knowledge that they were fellow Dutchmen ready and eager to help the enemy in their inhuman activities, made the situation still more unbearable.

After the war these men were sentenced to death for their participation in these activities. At the time I was in America and received the following letter from my sister:

> Willemsen and Kaptein have both been sentenced to be shot next week. Will you pray for their salvation? I have written them that there is still grace in the Lord Jesus, and that if they receive Him as their Savior and bring their sins to Him, He will forgive them. Jesus died for the sins of the whole world, theirs included; salvation is a gift: but they must accept it. I wrote them that their work with the enemy caused the death of Father, my sister Betsie, my brother Willem and his son Kik, and that we too had suffered in prison and concentration camp; but that we had forgiven them because we ourselves had received forgiveness from Jesus Christ when we had received Him as our Savior. I told them that our forgiveness was a very small example of His forgiveness for sinners, and that we would pray for them.

When I received this letter I was a guest at the Moody Bible Institute and read it in the office where my mail had been put. A friend who worked there walked past me just then, so I stopped her and told her the story of Willemsen and Kaptein. She promised to pray for their salvation and added, "I am just going to broadcast. Every week we have a prayer meeting over the air; many Christians tune in and pray for the requests we make. I will mention these two men."

So it happened that people all over America prayed for their salvation.

Eventually my sister received two letters: one from Willemsen and one from Kaptein. One wrote: "I know what I have done to the family ten Boom. That you and your sister could forgive me was for me the evidence that there is forgiveness in Jesus Christ. I have brought to Him my sins and received Him as my Savior."

The other wrote, "I know what I have done to the family ten Boom. Not only have I been the cause of your father's death and the death of other members of your family, but I have also helped to kill thousands of Jewish people. The only regret I have is that I was not able to kill more of your brood."

Two murderers died on crosses on either side of Jesus. One said to Jesus, "Lord remember me when thou comest into thy kingdom."

He received this reply: "To day shalt thou be with me in paradise" (Luke 23: 42, 43). The other blasphemed and died in his sins. One said "yes" to Jesus while the other said "no." What about you?

Dr. J. H. Jowett has said, "The blood of Jesus Christ can wash out blaspheming, adultery, fornication, lying, slander, perjury, theft, murder; though thou hast raked in the very kernel of hell, yet if thou wilt come to Christ and ask mercy, He will absolve thee from all sins."

SUNBEAMS IN PRISON

Let the beauty of the Lord our God be upon us. (Ps. 90:17)

In a prison in Wanganui in New Zealand, I was allowed to give a talk to fourteen criminals. A minister led the meeting, and with me was a singer who had brought a little folding harmonium with him, and two other Christians—a team of five for an attendance of fourteen.

I am always so happy to have an opportunity to speak to prisoners, for I know from experience how it feels to be behind a door that can be opened only from the outside. Nor do I feel any better than a criminal, for I know that it is by the grace of God that I am not one of them. I have hated, and hatred is murder in the eyes of God. When I brought my hatred to the Lord, He forgave and cleansed me; Jesus' blood does a good job. He gave even me love for my enemies.

So while I was speaking, I prayed that God's love should stream through me. It is so important that listeners should see the joy of the Lord on one's face. The Israelites, for example, were more impressed by the beaming face of Moses than by the Shekinah, the pillar of cloud and light. The Holy Spirit worked, and four prisoners trusted the Lord Jesus for salvation.

I shook hands with all fourteen. One of them, an old man who had been guilty of murder, cried when it came to his turn. His case was one of manslaughter, with a humorous as well as a very tragic side. One night the woman with whom he had been living snored so heavily that it made him furious. Being in a drunken stupor, not aware of what he was doing, he strangled her. When he saw what he had done he sobered up and ran to the police station. He was given a life sentence.

Holding tightly to my hand he sobbed. I asked, "Why do you cry?"

"I feel so happy because now I know that Jesus loves me."

"Praise the Lord. But now let me go!"

He kissed my hand and then let it go. A murderer kissed my hand—what an honor!

Later I sent a Bible correspondence course to the men with an encouraging letter which I signed, "Yours in Jesus the Victor, Corrie ten Boom." Three of the men, though not the old man, sent replies starting off with "Dear Corrie." It was rather like becoming their "girlfriend" by correspondence.

It was ten months before I could visit them again. When I did my pen-friends were happy and proud to meet me, asking many questions:

"Corrie, which countries have you seen?"

". . . and Corrie, where have you been since last year?"

They were eager to show their fellow prisoners that I was their girlfriend. I asked them, "Where is that old man who made his decision for the Lord?"

"He died suddenly, some time ago."

One of my "boyfriends" took me aside and said, "That man always called out to me when I was passing his cell, 'Come in and let us have a talk about Corrie's message.'"

There are moments in my life as a traveling tramp for the Lord when my cup runneth over with joy.

Not for myself I ask for power, Lord Jesus.
Rather to win the souls of men to Thee,
I give myself in reasonable service.
May I be Spirit-filled abundantly.

FELLOW SINNERS

[The people] which say, Stand by thyself, come not near to me;
for I am holier than thou. These are a smoke in my [God's] nose.
(Isa. 65:5)

I was in a prison in Honolulu where the men had built a pleasing chapel. So often I have been in church halls or rooms in prisons which were dirty and drab, but here everything was spick and span with clean, orderly seats and flowers on the altar table. We almost forgot that we were in a prison.

The men themselves took part in the service, one reading the Scriptures, one playing the organ and another leading the choir. It was one of the men who also had painted the notice—a little card with a neatly typed invitation to hear Miss Corrie ten Boom, who had "served her term in Germany."

I smiled when I read it. All the prisoners came to see their fellow criminal from Germany. I looked into my own heart. Was I shocked to find myself placed on the same level with them? No, I was not. Are not my decent little sins as great in the eyes of God as the crimes of men? Is it not only by the grace of God that I am not a criminal? I could hate, and indeed did hate, the people who were cruel to my beloved family. But hatred is murder. It was only because the Lord Jesus gave me love for my enemies that I was able to love, forgive and forget.

"Unto me, who am less than the least of all saints, is this grace given, that I should preach . . . the unsearchable riches of Christ" (Eph. 3:8). It was just because Paul was so perfectly assured of his acceptance and of his vocation that he felt so totally unworthy.

STRANDED

Make me a captive, Lord.

*This is a faithful saying, and worthy of all acceptation,
that Christ Jesus came into the world to save sinners;
of whom I am chief.* (1 Tim. 1:15)

In the Silliman University of Cebu in the Philippines, I met a group of students who sometimes worked in a small prison near the campus. One Sunday afternoon I was able to join them. We were allowed to go into a "by-cell," where many prisoners lived together, and found them sitting on the two-tiered bunks which were standing against the walls. The room was very dark, and as I was speaking a strong wind made the shutters bang open and shut. So the men closed them, with the result that I could scarcely see the faces of those around me.

What a place to live in! I could feel the presence of that great enemy of prisoners: boredom. One man lay on his bunk, seemingly asleep, while the rest stood leaning against or sitting on the edges of their bunks and listened while I told them about the Lord Jesus, the strong Friend, who loved them and had died for us all. I told them that when I was in the concentration camp His love and friendship were the greatest realities. He not only kept hatred out of my heart, but He even gave me love for my enemies.

The sleeping man opened his eyes and listened. After a few minutes he threw his legs over the edge of the bunk and leaned on his elbows, his head in his hands.

Gradually my eyes grew accustomed to the darkness, so that I could see the faces about me. There were several sins portrayed on those faces, but common to all was the expression of miserable failure. Sometimes in my dreams I see them again, and I thank God that I was able to tell them about the ocean of God's love in Jesus Christ. Every soul is precious in His eyes. Also, I was able to tell them how the sufferings which I had experienced during the war made me realize that when the worst happens in the life of a child of God, the best remains.

I knew that the students were praying. How much I count on the work of the Holy Spirit! In truth that dark room became a palace of light, for we felt the presence of the Lord.

"Friends, I must leave, but Jesus has said, 'Lo, I am with you alway.' Talk a lot with Him; and read this Book, the Bible, for it will tell you so much."

I mentioned the correspondence course which we could arrange for them to take if they were willing to study the Bible and asked those who were interested to give their names to two of the students while I visited in some other cells. When I asked the students later how many would be taking the course, they replied that all the men had given their names.

Shall I see them again? When I do, it will not be in a dark, dirty prison room but in a beautiful heaven where together we will praise Him who came to this world to "seek and to save that which was lost."

> *I know a Fount where sins are washed away;*
> *I know a place where night is turned to day;*
> *Burdens are lifted, blind eyes made to see;*
> *There's a wonder-working pow'r in the blood of Calvary.*

Four

Japanese Jottings

*If we are sitting on Peter's chair, and we are no Peter,
we peter out.* (Rufus Moseley)

*Be careful that nobody spoils your faith through intellectualism
or high-sounding nonsense.* (Col. 2:8, Phillips)

In many countries it is necessary for me to have the help of
interpreters. Speaking thus, "around the corner," can sometimes be the cause of certain loss of contact with my listeners. Therefore the personality of the interpreter is very important. If he, or she, is not a channel of the living water,
then we cannot expect blessing. I always try to have a chat
with him before we stand on the platform together.

While in Japan a college professor was appointed once
to be my interpreter. I invited him to visit me beforehand in
order that he might become acquainted with my accent and
with my speaking technique and that I might find out if he
were a Christian.

"Is it a long time since you received Jesus as your Savior?"
I asked.

"I have never done so and do not intend to, either. There
is so much in the Bible that I cannot understand, and I see

so many Christians leaving churches in Japan."

This indeed is a sad truth. The enemy is very active in Japan, as scores of Christians leave the churches and turn back to heathenism.

"I am so sorry but I cannot use you as my interpreter. You cannot talk about the gospel if you do not believe it yourself. If you were to sell watches or fish believing them to be inferior, not good enough for yourself, you would not do much business."

"But I will faithfully interpret what you say. Many missionaries have used me and nobody has complained."

"I am sorry," I replied firmly. "Talking about the gospel brings you on to sacred ground. You can only be used when you are open for the Holy Spirit. But why do you not trust the Lord Jesus as your Savior? It is such a joy to know Him!"

I prayed with him and promised to continue in prayer for him that he might be able and willing to receive the Lord Jesus as his Savior.

In the evening he came back, saying, "Miss ten Boom, I can be your interpreter. I have accepted Christianity."

"But I still cannot use you. If you believe in Communism, you are a Communist; if you believe in Shintoism, you are a Shintoist; but belief in Christianity offers no evidence that you are a Christian. Christianity is a person—Jesus Christ. Accept Him; bring your sins to Him; and He will make you a Christian. And how He loves you!"

Again I prayed with him. The following day he returned and said with joy:

"I can be your interpreter. I have received Him, Jesus Christ. Please tell me the next step."

He was busy telling the "next steps" to others during the

whole week when he interpreted for me. Later I learned that many people had been praying for him for a long time.

> Only spiritual life can exist in heaven. Your dog cannot understand your sorrow because it has animal life. If it had human life, it could. You cannot enjoy fellowship with God because you have human life. We need to be born again to have spiritual life. (Oswald J. Smith)

THE JAPANESE PROFESSOR

Realize that you have sinned and get your hands clean again.
(James 4:8, Phillips)

In Japan I had such a problem! When I first arrived all the faces looked so very much alike. I distinguished about six different types and fitted them into one of these groups. (I have heard it said that the Japanese find the same difficulty when they come to Europe.) It is a good thing that God can bless even our blunders.

Each week during my visit there, I had to speak at three different places: a seminary, an I.V.F. group and a university group where there were very few Christians. Speaking to the I.V.F. group one day, I saw a gentleman enter and, thinking he was the director from the seminary, I asked him to pray with us at the close of the meeting. His answer was: "But I have never prayed before. I wouldn't know how to go about it!"

Immediately I saw my error; he was a professor at the heathen university. I prayed myself. At the close of the meeting the professor came over to me. After bowing three times in the polite Japanese fashion, he said, "I am so sorry I was unable to do as you asked, but I am not a Christian and do not know how to pray."

"I honor you for your refusal. Perhaps some people would have said a prayer without really believing it, but you were too honest for that. I appreciate it very much. But tell me, why are you not a Christian?"

"To become a Christian I must first study Christianity."

"But here in this book, the Bible, it is not written that those who by studying Christianity receive power to become children of God but that those who receive its Truth, Jesus, become His children through the power He gives to them (John 1:12). I showed him the way of salvation, and very shortly he made his decision which causes the angels to rejoice. Just then John Schwab, the director of the I.V.F. group, passed our room, and I invited him in.

"Can you tell Mr. Schwab what you have done?"

"But he knows the way of salvation! I don't have to tell him!"

"That is so, but I'd like to hear you testify to your faith now."

"Oh, now I understand. Mr. Schwab, I have just received Jesus as my Savior. He has made me a child of God."

"I'll be happy to show you the next steps," John answered, and made an appointment for a weekly Bible study.

What a blessed mistake I made! In the hand of God it led to the salvation of that professor, a man with a strategic position in that university.

It is just like this story. At a weavers' school one of the students was asked by a visitor, "What happens if you make a mistake? Do you cut everything out and begin afresh?"

"No," was the reply. "Our master is such an artist that he

often uses our mistakes to improve the beauty of the pattern."

As Dr. J. H. Jowett has written:

I suppose it is true of all preachers that as we grow older our sense of the inefficiency of our work becomes intensified. The wonder grows that God can accomplish so much with such inadequate implements. One's satisfaction with the Evangel deepens with the years; but one is increasingly discontented with the imperfect way in which we present it. No, I do not write as one who is proficient. I am only a blunderer at best; but I write as one who is honestly desirous of better and more useful equipment.

Two Heroes

I complained because I had no shoes; then I saw a man without feet and I complained no longer. (Chinese proverb)

The night cometh, when no man can work. (John 9:4)

In another of my meetings in Japan a man whose legs were paralyzed had been brought to the little church in his wheelchair. His face wore a very happy expression; and when I asked him about the little package on his lap, he showed me how he had written the whole Gospel of John in Braille— the raised script of the blind.

"I can do this work for the Master and send gospels and other portions of the Bible to many blind people."

"How did you get this idea?"

"Well, our Bible woman is very ill with tuberculosis, but she travels every week to several villages. And so I said to God, 'Lord, I must help her. Although my legs are para-

lyzed, I am healthier than she is; so please show me what I
can do.' I believe when we ask for such things, God gives the
guidance we need.

"One day I read an advertisement in the paper request-
ing somebody to do this work for the blind. I volunteered,
learned Braille, and now I can work for the Master by giving
these people a chance to read the Bible. My eyes are very
healthy, and these poor blind people miss so much."

I myself have met the Bible woman of whom he spoke;
the occasion being a memorable one. I was feeling tired and
downhearted at the time as a result of many little inconve-
niences such as the hot and humid climate, which can be
very difficult in Japan, and the problem presented by the
food. I was not accustomed to these strange dishes and had
not been able to find a place where European food was served.
These and other small discomforts were filling me with self-
pity. Then I met the Bible woman: a woman with tuberculosis in both lungs, whose face showed only too graphically
how the illness was consuming her frail body.

"Can you not go to bed?" I asked her.

She smiled bravely and replied, "I cannot stay in bed;
there is so much work to do. There are many places here-
abouts where people have never heard the gospel. I have the
Bible, and in it is food for everyone. There are many who are
hungry, and many who know they are sinners but don't know
what to do about it. From the Bible they learn that Jesus
Christ is the answer, for He is the only One who can save
and cleanse them and satisfy their hearts. He brings them
from darkness to light and He has plenty for them all. With
so many to help, how then can I go to bed? No, I shall go on
working for as long as I may."

"In how many villages do you work?"

"Every week I visit sixteen villages, and I train young people in this work so that they can reach places where I cannot go."

My self-pity had disappeared, and I thanked God that I had met two of His heroes.

"The work of feeding and tending sheep is hard work," wrote Oswald Chambers, "arduous work, and love for the sheep alone will not do it; you must have a consuming love for the Great Shepherd, the Lord Jesus Christ. Then He will flow through you in a passion of love and draw men to Himself."

STREET EVANGELISM

Towards non-Christians . . . speak pleasantly.
(Col. 4:5, Phillips)

For the Son of man is come to seek and to save that which was lost.
(Luke 19:10)

I had been in Japan for only four days when I met Mr. and Mrs. Mitchell at the home of their son-in-law, David Morken. The Mitchells have seven children, all of whom are on the mission field, and with them they started the "Go Ye Fellowship," which now has many more missionaries all over the world. When I met them in Japan, they were on their way to visit and encourage those special messengers, their own missionaries. Seldom have I seen such happy children of God.

They had arrived a week before me, and Mrs. Mitchell had learned to say "Good morning" in Japanese: "O-hi-yogo-

sa-i-mas." One day a young woman who often worked as
interpreter paid us a visit. Mrs. Mitchell asked her if she had
time to go with her for a walk, that perhaps they could do
some work for the Master. It was agreed and I joined them,
thus being privileged to witness a little piece of street evan-
gelism such as I had never seen before.

In a back street a dirty, little Japanese woman with a baby
on her back came towards us. Mrs. Mitchell greeted her with,
"O-hi-yo go-sa-i-mas." The little woman smiled. It was four
o'clock in the afternoon!

"Do you know," Mrs. Mitchell continued, "that I have a
Friend who is so good to me, and helps me always, just when
I need Him? And you know He will be your friend too. . . ."

The little woman listened intently while the interpreter
translated as Mrs. Mitchell went on to tell her about Jesus
and His love for us. Suddenly she said to the interpreter,
"My little house is over here. Can I talk with you alone?"

Together they went into the dirty little house while Mrs.
Mitchell and I stayed outside and prayed, "Oh Lord, use
this conversation, and use the interpreter to bring this woman
to the great decision. Lay your hand on her life."

They remained inside for a long time, but at last the
interpreter came out to us, her face beaming with joy, and
said, "She trusts the Lord Jesus for salvation. I felt that you
were both praying for us and that the Lord was working in
her heart. She truly has come into His glorious freedom, but
please continue praying for her; she will need it."

Then she told us the story of the little woman. Her husband was a drunkard, and although he had a good job in the
employ of a Christian man, he had been "fired" only the day
before because of his misbehavior. The little house was very

dirty. The wife, in a state of frustration and defeat through these experiences, had long ago lost all incentive or desire to keep it clean. She had, in fact, been on her way to commit suicide with her baby when God had brought about this meeting with Mrs. Mitchell.

David Morken went that very day to see the husband and had the joy of bringing him to the Lord. Then finding the Christian employer, he persuaded him to give this man another chance. A month later when he next visited the couple, they found the house and baby clean, and the little woman—why, she was full of praise to the Lord!

PIONEERING

Pray that . . . I may make that mystery plain to men. . . .
(Col. 4:4, Phillips)

Before the outbreak of the Second World War, I had a Bible class for feeble-minded people. (This work is described in a booklet I wrote, *Common-sense Not Needed*.) During that time I learned that backward people in my hometown were not really reached with the gospel. Yet the gospel is for everyone, as Jesus died for the sins of the whole world. We who have able minds need the Holy Spirit to show us how to understand spiritual things. Is the Holy Spirit, therefore, unable to reach a person with a low intelligence quotient? He does not need our common sense to reveal Himself. Thus it was a great joy to see how many of these poor ones became happy Christians. They could never hear enough of the wonderful love of God.

The work done among these people trained me for

spreading the gospel in the prison camps during the war, where many had never before heard of the Lord Jesus. It was borne upon me too in the work that I have since done all over the world that many people need a very simple message.

A young missionary in Japan invited me to go with her to a village where no missionary had ever been. A Japanese friend of hers, when he heard the plans was enthusiastic and promised to print and distribute leaflets in the village concerned. He even promised to rent the theater for the meeting. When we arrived in the village, however, we found no theater had been rented and no leaflets given out; nobody knew of our coming at all. We asked if we might rent the theater ourselves, but the keys were nowhere to be found.

While waiting for a boy who tried to find out for us, we were surrounded by many children who looked with curiosity at these ladies with their strange white faces. At last help arrived. A man told us that the keys could not be found, but he knew another way in. The directness of his approach to the problem was fascinating: he merely pushed his shoulder against the thin wall which obligingly gave way, and we entered the very large and dusty hall. Seating myself on the platform, I invited all the children to sit in front of me. Just then some women started to sweep the floor. Through the resulting cloud of dust, I saw people enter and seat themselves around the walls.

My interpreter and I raised our voices so that everyone could hear us, all the while looking at the children in front but aware that the many grown-ups in the background were listening intently. I told them how God loves us and that He has a beautiful place, heaven, where He makes room for everyone. But the bad people, God has said, have to be punished. Once He had a talk with His Son, Jesus, and said, "I love the people on earth so much, but they cannot come to Me because they are so evil and have done so many wrong things. I must punish them. If only there were someone to take their punishment, then I could forgive them."

Jesus replied, "Father, I love them too. How would it be if I went to the earth to bear their sins and punishment, so that they can find a way to heaven through Me?"

"And," I continued, "that is just what He did. He died on the cross, and everyone who believes in Him will not perish but have everlasting life in heaven. Jesus is the Way, and I have a Book here that says a great deal about Him."

After the talk many of the grown-ups came to us and bought Bibles. While we were selling them and distributing tracts, our Japanese friend arrived with his leaflets—a little bit late. But I believe that angels had done the job, for we certainly had had a full church that day.

Complications come from the devil and ourselves. Are we too grown up to take the gospel simply and to follow His guiding? But though the truth is so simple in the Bible, it is so deep that we need the help of the Holy Spirit to understand it that we might know Jesus and His ways.

Five

Island Itinerary

One day, when he shows himself in full splendour to men, you will be filled with the most tremendous joy. (1 Pet. 4:13, Phillips)

In Hong Kong the state has erected huge concrete buildings in order to house the hundreds of thousands of refugees who pour in. There are so many children among them that the schools cannot open their doors to them.

The Oriental Missionary Society is doing a splendid work there—the "roof-top mission" being a very important part of what they do. Here they gather the children together every day on the flat roofs of the huge buildings to give them Bible teaching and as much of the usual school curriculum they are able to give. Many of the teachers are young converts from among the refugees themselves. Also helping to swell the numbers of the large staff are lawyers, business men and indeed anyone who is educated and willing to serve the Lord in this way.

I was able to spend a week with these workers, most of whom were still young Christians. One day we were discussing the joy of the Lord's return to earth. A young lawyer said, "I must confess that I am a bit afraid of His coming. I am still a babe in Christ, and there is much of which I am ashamed."

"Don't you know what to do with your sins?"

"Yes, confess them, and the blood of Jesus cleanses us from all sin" (see 1 John 1:7–9).

"Isn't that the answer? If we are instant in prayer in bringing our sins to the Lord, the blood of Jesus cleanses us and we can be ready with a clean heart to meet the Lord in the air. 'Abide in him; that, when he shall appear, we may have confidence, and not be ashamed before him at his coming' (1 John 2:28)."

This reminded me of the time when my sister Betsie and I were arrested. They pushed her into a cell of the prison and, looking at me over the shoulder of the guard, she called back, "Corrie, if Jesus should come again now, they will find our cells empty."

What did she mean? She was obeying the command of 1 Thessalonians 4:18 where, after the message on the translation of the church, Paul says that he has a definite word from the Lord: "So by all means use this message to encourage one another" (Phillips). What a comfort indeed it proved to be to me when I was in solitary confinement for four months.

What a joy to know that "the best is yet to be," and if Jesus tarries yet we know that one day He *will* come, and we shall see Him face to face. I long for that day to come. Why? Because I love Him.

My father was a very dear man and, I believe, the best father anyone could have in the whole world. He often had to go away on business, and although we were not sure when he would return, flowers were placed in his room every day. Oh, the joy when he did return home! My place at the oval dinner table was opposite his, which meant that I could look into his eyes. With these lovely eyes and a long beard, he had just the sort of face I imagined a patriarch would have. Why was I so happy? Because I loved him.

There is fear in the heart of a disobedient servant when the master returns, but there is joy in the heart of an obedient child when the father comes home. How I should love it if Jesus should come today. Just imagine how wonderful it would be not to have to be sick, to die or to pass through the valley of the shadow of death.

> *O joy, O delight, should we go without dying;*
> *No sickness, no sorrow, no sadness, no crying;*
> *Caught up in the clouds to meet Him in glory,*
> *When Jesus receives His own.*

I am not afraid of the valley of the shadow of death. I have often been close to it, yet I know that my Redeemer lives and that He has made me a child of God. I gave Him my heart and He has promised, "You must not let yourselves be distressed—you must hold on to your faith in God and to your faith in me. There are many rooms in my Father's House. If there were not, should I have told you that I am going away to prepare a place for you?" (John 14:1–2, Phillips).

My experiences really do enable me to say, "O death, where is thy sting?" (1 Cor. 15:55). Death is not a pit, but a tunnel. I know that when I die, I shall immediately see my Lord; for did He not say to the thief on the cross, "To day shalt thou be with me in paradise" (Luke 23:43)?

Not only are my sins forgiven by Jesus whom I love so much and a place is prepared in heaven by Him for me, but there is a third reason why I pray with all my heart, "Come soon, Jesus!" That is the suffering which exists throughout

the whole world. How terrible a prospect is the amount of
sickness, of the unnatural, shut-in lives of prisoners and of
people who are mentally ill. Oh, the many tears that there
are in the world. Think too for what the nations are preparing: the next war. Then compare all this with the promises
in the Bible:

> They shall beat their swords into plowshares. (Mic. 4:3)
>
> God himself shall be with them, and will wipe away
> every tear from their eyes. Death shall be no more, and never
> again shall there be sorrow or crying or pain. (Rev. 21:3–4,
> Phillips)

Most of all I long for that blessed time because I read in
the Bible about the longing father-heart of God: "O that
there were such an heart in them, that they would fear me,
and keep all my commandments always, that it might be
well with them, and with their children for ever!" (Deut. 5:29).

That time will come when Jesus has done what He promised in Revelation 21: "See, I am making all things new."
Then the "earth shall be filled with the knowledge of the
glory of the Lord, as the waters cover the sea" (Hab. 2:14).
What joy must be God's when this happens, for He loves
the world. When the three agree—the Spirit, the Bride and
he who hears (see Rev. 22:17)—then Jesus will say, "Yes, I
am coming quickly . . . Amen, come, Lord Jesus!" (Rev. 22:20,
Phillips). Yes, "the best is yet to be."

THE URGENCY OF JESUS' SECOND COMING

We are citizens of heaven; our outlook goes beyond this world to
the hopeful expectation of the Savior who will come from heaven,
the Lord Jesus Christ. (Phil. 3:20, Phillips)

In a home in Korea we had a meeting with the leaders of a campaign. During our discussion about the program, I suggested that I should speak about the world's great coming event: Jesus' return. One pastor said, "We do not expect only Christians to the meeting, but also a number of unsaved people. Is it so important to speak to them about Jesus' coming again? Only mature people of God are interested in that message."

I could not agree with this statement so replied, "I believe that also the unsaved can be stirred by it, for the world is very pessimistic about what is going to happen next. They do not know what is coming, but we know *who* is coming. 'For God has allowed us to know the secret of his plan, and it is this: he purposes in his sovereign will that all human history shall be consummated in Christ, that everything that exists in heaven or earth shall find its perfection and fulfilment in him. And here is the staggering thing—that in all which will one day belong to him we have been promised a share . . .' (Eph. 1:9–11, Phillips). It is such a tremendous privilege to know God's plan and, knowing what the future will be, must we keep the truth to ourselves? One out of every twenty-five texts in the Bible concerns the second coming of Jesus, which makes us realize that the Holy Spirit regards it as very important. We must therefore tell others about it."

It was agreed. I decided to use as an illustration the story of a little girl and her desk. One day a visitor came to her school and, seeing all the desks were very untidy, he said to the children, "When I return I will give a prize to the child who has the tidiest desk."

"I'm going to have that prize," said this little girl. The whole class laughed, for she had the untidiest desk of them all.

"How will you manage that?" asked one of the others.

"I'll clean my desk every Monday morning."

"And what if he comes on Friday. I'm afraid by then it will be untidy again."

"Yes, that's true. Well, I'll clean my desk every morning."

"But what if he comes at three o'clock?"

The little girl thought for a moment and then made up her mind, "I'll just *keep* my desk *clean*."

That evening God had given me the following verse to preach on: "Because, my dear friends, you have a hope like this before you, I urge you to make certain that such a day would find you at peace with God and man, clean and blameless in his sight" (2 Pet. 3:14, Phillips).

After reading the passage I said, "We do not know which day or hour Jesus will return, but we do not know of any day or hour when He can not come. If He should come tonight, how would He find you? With bitterness in your heart or in the midst of a church quarrel? Forgiving your enemies—or not? 'Watch therefore, for ye know neither the day nor the hour wherein the Son of man cometh' (Matt. 25:13).

"And what about you who have rejected Jesus Christ? There is a question nobody can answer. If all the professors in the world and all the angels in heaven were gathered here, they could not answer it. In Hebrews 2:3 (Phillips) it says, 'How shall we escape if we refuse to pay proper attention to the salvation that is offered us today?'

"When He does come it will be a terrible day for the unsaved. They will call for the rocks and the mountains to fall on them and to hide them from the wrath of His divine judgment' (Rev. 6:16). In Hebrews 3:7 it says, 'To day if ye will hear his voice, Harden not your hearts.' What then can we do? How can we prepare ourselves for this event? Again the Bible gives us God's answer, 'Live . . . in him so that if he were suddenly to reveal himself we should still know exactly where we stand, and should not have to shrink away from his presence" (1 John 2:28, Phillips). We have but to surrender to Jesus Himself and He Himself will keep us and prepare us for His coming. As Philippians 1:6 affirms, 'He which hath begun a good work in you will perform it until the day of Jesus Christ.'"

> May the God of peace make you holy through and through. May you be kept in soul and mind and body in spotless integrity until the coming of our Lord Jesus Christ. (1 Thess. 5:23, Phillips)

PREDESTINATION

Life from nothing began through him,
and life from the dead began through him. (Col. 1:18, Phillips)

On one of the small islands of the Philippines, there is a beautiful university, the Silliman University, where I was invited to take some meetings. One evening I was delighted to find some of the time was to be devoted to answering questions of the various members of the group of students who would be attending. This is something I like very much. It is enlightening to hear what problems there are and it also increases one's knowledge and consequently one's ability to make platform talks more relevant and practical.

One of the young men asked, "I read in Ephesians 1 that we are chosen 'before the foundation of the world.' Does that mean that God has predestined us a long time ago? Then why worry? If I'm elected I'll be saved. If I'm not, I cannot do anything against the will of a mighty God."

Another boy added, "Yes, but it is also written, 'Work out your own salvation with fear and trembling. For it is God which worketh in you both to will and do of his good pleasure.'"

I prayed for His wisdom that I might give the right answer. Their problem was one that crops up every time men use their *sense*-knowledge to understand the Bible. After a few moments I spoke, "In Phillips' translation the verse you mention says, 'So then, my dearest friends, as you have always followed my advice—and that not only when I was present to give it—so now that I am far away be keener than ever to work out the salvation that God has given you with a proper sense of awe and responsibility. For it is God who is at work within you, giving you the will and the power to achieve his purpose' (Phil. 2:12–13).

"The truth is to be found not in one extreme or the other, nor in the compromise between the two, but in the two extremes. In First Corinthians, chapters 1 and 2, you read there that there are two realms: the wisdom of the wise and the foolishness of God. We arrive at the first with our logical thought by our knowledge through the senses, but we grasp the truth of God's foolishness only by knowledge through faith. We cannot bring down the greatest wisdom, namely the foolishness of God, into the realm of the wisdom of the wise, but the Holy Spirit teaches us to lift up the wisdom of the wise—knowledge through the *senses*—into the realms of the foolishness of God. There you find the reality, the vision."

"But first I have to understand before I can believe."

"That is logical when looked at from the world's viewpoint, but where the things of God are concerned the opposite applies. First believe; then understand. Act on the Word of God—-the Bible—and you will experience that God means what He says when He gave us these promises."

"I feel that my faith is rather small."

"Hudson Taylor said, 'It is not a great faith that we need, but faith in a great God.' Jesus said that even if our faith is small as a grain of mustard seed, it can remove mountains. I saw great faith among the Nazis during the war, but it was in the wrong person. When the jailer at Philippi asked Paul, 'What must I do to be saved?' the answer was: 'Believe on the Lord Jesus Christ, and thou shalt be saved.' When you take this step, then the Holy Spirit witnesses with your spirit that you are a child of God.

Here you are using the joyful cooperation of the two extremes: We are on the Lord's side at the very moment we enter through the door of faith. This is the great beginning of the fight of faith, and we need the armor of God so that we may stand our ground in the evil day, even when we have come to a standstill. But it is a fight of victory from the position of victory towards victory. The Lord throws wide open the door of faith's treasure-house of plenty and bids us enter and take with boldness."

"A lady once said to F. B. Meyer, 'I believe that God does everything in me, and for me.' To which F. B. Meyer replied, 'Does He read the Bible for you?'"

The doctrine of predestination is meant by God to be a great comfort and security. In the hands of the devil it can make us confused. Many have heard from the platform the parable about predestination. You enter the gate of salvation on which is written, "Come unto me, all . . .", but once inside, if you glance back, you read on the lintel, "Chosen . . . in him before the foundation of the world." Both extremes! The foolishness of God is not understandable, but how much higher than the wisdom of the wise.

Is a Small Number Important

There is joy in the presence of the angels of God
over one sinner that repenteth. (Luke 15:10)

I was in the beautiful Hawaiian Islands having a very busy time with many meetings to attend—in clubs, student groups, homes and churches. The days became more and more crowded; the weather was warm; I felt tired. An old lady offered me the use of her beach cottage so that I could rest for a few days. She was unable to stay with me in the cottage at that time, so I was left alone to enjoy the peace and quiet. The Lord always knows what we need: what a blessing it was to me to hear nothing for a little while except the eternal song of the sea.

It was an old house and the termites had had a grand time in the freedom of the uninhabited building. They had eaten their way not only through a bundle of books and papers but also through the table as well. I also had the company of some rats and mice. Fortunately I managed to find an upstairs room which gave me some measure of privacy.

On my first morning at the cottage, I was greeted by one of the neighbors who knocked at the door and brought me some eggs. She too was a missionary and kindly offered me help if any need arose. I had already noticed that she had visitors in her garden; she told me that they came every week for a Bible study.

"I am sure you are not willing to sacrifice a morning of your vacation to bring them a message . . ." she ventured.

I looked at the small number of people seated around the table in her garden. Only seven! Was it worth going? Suddenly I remembered how Jesus had devoted a long evening to only one man, a man who would not come to him during the day; and what a talk He gave him! (John 3:1–21). If the Lord Jesus thought Nicodemus important enough to give him one of His most inspiring and enlightening talks, was it right for me to refuse to give a morning to seven ladies? Jesus went seventy miles out of His way to meet the Samaritan woman. . . .

"Surely, I will come," I promised.

And what a good time we had in that beautiful garden by the beach near Honolulu! We sat beneath a blossoming tree with the song of the sea as an accompaniment to my voice.

During my talk I mentioned to them how I was tested on one occasion in New Zealand. When the only way for me to get to a certain meeting was to hire a private airplane, I had said, "Lord, I will cancel that meeting. To go by private plane will cost too much money."

But the Lord had replied, "If one soul is saved or one Christian awakened it will be worth more than a million pounds."

Now as I spoke to these seven, I told them that more than ever I realized how precious every soul is in the eyes of God.

While we were enjoying the coffee which my missionary neighbor served us afterwards, one lady said to me, "You owe me a million."

"What do you mean?" I queried.

"You said that one soul is worth more than a million. During your talk I accepted Jesus Christ as my Savior."

"Praise the Lord! I had understood that all of you were already saved: real Christians. How many of you know that you are children of God?" I asked as I turned to the rest. All but two of them raised their hands. I asked one of these, "Aren't you willing to receive Jesus Christ as your Savior?"

"No, I can't. I have so many terrible difficulties in my life. You would understand if you knew all about them."

"But, whatever your difficulties are, you need a Savior and Friend. Perhaps more than anyone else. If you bring your problems and sins to Him, you will find what a Friend we can have in Jesus." I showed her that after we have surrendered to Jesus, He takes the steering-wheel of the car of our lives and drives through all the dangers with a strong and steady hand. Then she, too, said her "Yes" to Jesus.

The second lady promised, "I'll make a decision later. There is plenty of time."

"Is there? Let me tell you a legend I once read. In the story Satan planned to send one of his servants into the world to deceive people. One devil said, 'Send me; I will convince people that God and the devil are merely products of human fantasy.' The second said, 'Send me; I will convince people that the Bible is not true.' While a third spoke, 'Send me; I will tell them that neither heaven nor hell exists and that life ends with death.' But the fourth offered, 'I think you can send me with great confidence. I'll tell them that the Bible is true, that God and the devil exist, that there are only two alternatives for eternity—heaven or hell—but there is no hurry at all to decide.' The last received the job and it is he who has inspired you to postpone your decision. But you may be sure that he is a liar, for you can be saved in God's time and not in yours. I do not say that there is no possibility of another time, but this could be the last time."

She also accepted the Lord. How glad I was that I had given my vacation morning to this meeting of seven ladies!

UNMARRIED

To those who love God, . . . everything that happens fits into a pattern for good. (Rom. 8:28, Phillips)

What heroes I have met among missionaries. There are some in the islands of the Far East who make trips through the jungles—sometimes walking for two or three weeks at a time, or paddling a canoe and then carrying it when the rapids are reached. They forge their trail through the jungle to reach far-flung little tribal settlements. Here they will spend a few weeks "Bible teaching" before setting out on another long trek to visit the next group.

I am so happy when God uses me to encourage some of these special messengers of His. I have often seen how the enemy tries in so many subtle ways to spoil the peace and joy they have in their work. Although the devil is not omnipresent, he has a good secret service to help him, with six thousand years of practice in tempting God's children.

One of the means he uses, I discovered as I have chatted with different lady missionaries, is the frustration of remaining unmarried. I was asked by one why I myself had never married.

"Because," I said, "the Lord had other plans for me than married life."

"Were you always willing for it to be so?" she continued.

"No, I wasn't, and I had to fight a battle over it. I was twenty-three when I began to understand that God was not willing to give me a husband. I loved a boy and believed he loved me. But I had no money and he married a rich girl. When he put her hand in mine and said, 'I hope you two will be friends,' I felt beaten.

"I went straight to the Source of the peace that passes understanding and said, 'Lord Jesus, you know that I belong to you one hundred per cent, and my sex life is yours too. I don't know what plans you have for my life, but Lord, whatever it may be—married or single—use me to realize your victory in every detail. You can take away all the frustrations and feelings of unhappiness. I surrender anew my whole to you!'

"Did that end the battle? No, not immediately, but it was a short battle and Jesus was the Victor.

"If you expect great things from Him, He does great things for you. My experience has been that the same energy required by women for their married life I have been able to use in giving the gospel to others, and that has truly satisfied my heart."

"Perhaps you are different from me. Although I do work to give the gospel to others, there always is in my heart a longing for married life."

"In Romans 12:1 Paul says, 'Present your bodies a living sacrifice . . . unto God.' The Lord never takes something away without giving something better in return. Surrender is such a joy! In surrender we become yoke-fellows with Jesus, and although it is costly to accept, it is far more costly to miss it. When you lose your life for Jesus' sake, it really means you are gaining it.'

"I believe you are right. After all, one sees many unhappy marriages."

"That's true. While marriage is a joyful thing for a woman, an unhappy one can be the source of terrible suffering. It is far better to be single than live in such a position as that. But this is only a natural and human answer to this problem; it is the sacrifice, the surrendering to the Lord Jesus that will take you into the realms of victory, of joy and of peace that passes understanding.

"Let me give you a little illustration of how some Christians see the reality and others do not: I was doing some hospital visiting and asked a patient who was a Christian and not very ill if he was ready to die.

"'Yes, I am,' he replied. 'Life is not worth while. I have suffered a lot of pain, and hospital life is dreary.'

"I turned to the man in the next bed and asked him the same question.

"'Yes, I am,' he answered. 'What joy is awaiting me! I'll see Jesus face to face. I am going to the house of my Father with its many mansions.' This Christian saw reality.

"We do not surrender to the Lord because there is nothing left but Him, rather because it is a great joy to jump into the ocean of God's love. When an empty bottle is thrown in the ocean it immediately is filled with and surrounded by the water. When Christians surrender to Jesus Christ, they are filled with and surrounded by God's love, knowing joy unspeakable and full of glory. It means getting progressively more acquainted with Jesus Christ Himself, and what a wonderful Savior He is.

"Do you think that God can use frustrated Christians or

those who are willing to accept His plans for their lives? The Holy Spirit will make us channels of living water. The Bible says that out of our innermost being will stream rivers of living water. Don't you think that rebelling against God's guidance can block the channel of your life?"

"Yes, I see it."

"Now, will you do it?"

"Do what?"

"Surrender your frustration, your problem, your lack in your life to the Lord Jesus?"

She surrendered her frustration; there was victory.

HUMBLING EXPERIENCE

If my people, which are called by my name, shall humble themselves, and pray, and turn from their wicked ways; then I will hear from heaven, and will forgive their sin, and will heal their land.
(2 Chron. 7:14)

On my way to fulfill a month-long speaking engagement in a Far Eastern country, I was delayed by a young man who requested that I stop off in his own town to plan for a week of meetings before going to my original destination.

"The town of K—— needs some help," he urged. "There are many Christians but much division among the various denominations. I pray God will use you to bring the churches together." He promised to make all the arrangements, including informing a friend of his who would be willing as host and cabling the mission director in the other town that I would be a few days late.

I saw the kind hand of the Lord in this meeting and

went full of courage to K——. When I arrived at the airport, however, no one was there to meet me. So I telephoned to the address which I had been given and asked how I might reach their home. "Take a taxi!" was the brief reply.

Upon my arrival I found a family who were very kind but who had not been informed that I was coming. Meanwhile a missionary plane was waiting in vain on the other side of the island to carry out my former plans. Arrangements were awry as Satan had sabotaged.

Happily we were able to straighten everything out. My host was most co-operative in taking me as his guest once the situation was explained and we were able to send a message to the pilot of the plane.

Then we began to work on the program for the campaign to be held in a month's time. My host told me that I would be able to work with his church, but he was sure that the other denominations, being spiritually dead, would not help, so they had not been invited.

"But," I said, "don't you think that we could give them a try? Let us invite one or two from each church and talk it over with them." After much discussion he agreed, though much against his will.

The meeting proved a surprise. The Salvation Army officer promised to open her hall for prayer meetings for all denominations between the hours of twelve noon and one-thirty every day. A man from another church agreed to hold himself responsible for the advertising. Altogether things seemed to be working out very well indeed.

Three weeks later I returned from my trip to the other side of this island for the campaign. My host and hostess, who had been counselors at Billy Graham meetings, had had counseling papers duplicated and then had distributed them among the counselors. There was a good attendance at the meetings; yet, although the Holy Spirit worked, no great blessing came. While my host and hostess were good to me, all the time I was conscious of a certain reserve towards me: I feared that I must have been tactless in some way.

On the last day of the campaign, the bomb burst. My hostess said, "I have nothing against Billy Graham or Major Thomas but I have much against you. Tell me, do you always arrive in places and say, 'Here I am!' and leave all the work involved for other people to do? I know that you have brought people to the Lord but who has to do the follow-up work? You go on and leave us the job."

I was beaten. I could have defended myself by pointing out that being let down by a young man in the first place (who had promised much) had gotten things off to a bad start; or that coming back to K—— for this week had involved me in extra expense, and so on. But I do not believe that Christians should vindicate themselves. Was I not promised in Exodus 14:14, "The Lord shall fight for you, and ye shall hold your peace"?

I said nothing but going to my room pleaded with the Lord. "What must I do, Lord? I have to stand on the platform with these very people who are so against me. How can we form a team? What must I do?"

I opened my Bible and read Matthew 5:23–24: "Therefore if thou bring thy gift to the altar, and there rememberest that thy brother hath ought against thee; Leave there thy gift before the altar, and go thy way; first be reconciled to thy brother, and then come and offer thy gift." Yes, my brother had something against me, but it was not my fault. Why did

Jesus ask this of us? Would it not be fairer to say, "If you have something against your brother"?

But disagreeing with a verse does not change the words of the Bible. I pleaded with the Lord, "Must I go to them and say 'I am sorry'?"

His answer was, "Humble yourself; the living water only streams through the lowest places." What an answer!

Chastened, I went to my host and hostess and said, "Will you forgive me for coming to this place?" Graciously they agreed, yet I have honestly to admit that I felt miserable.

Before the meeting I spoke to one of the team about it. He told me that he was expecting great blessing. "Before Billy Graham had his huge campaign in New York," he said, "the enemy managed to send great difficulties and attacks. And what blessing followed!" We prayed together and all feeling of depression left me.

That evening the Holy Spirit broke through; souls were saved and Christians came to repentance and total surrender. Afterwards my host and hostess shook hands with me and said, "You have not done wrong in coming."

Ever since that campaign prayer meetings are held each week in K——, being attended by people from all denominations. How good it is that the Lord has not changed Matthew 5:23–24. It is only we ourselves who can rob ourselves of His blessing. The faults and failures of others are no hindrance to God using us. Someone has said that Aaron's rod budded and blossomed even though it was tied up in a bundle of dry old sticks (see Num. 17:6–8).

Six

Zealous in New Zealand

Love knows no limit to its endurance, no end to its trust,
no fading of its hope; it can outlast anything. It is, in fact,
the one thing that still stands when all else has fallen.
(1 Cor. 13:7, Phillips)

"How can I bring my husband to the Lord?" a lady asked me in New Zealand. She was a true child of God, but she did not yet know that there are dozens of promises in the Bible. "When I am in the same room with him," she continued, "it is sometimes as though a cloud of darkness overshadows me."

"Act God's love," I told her. "In Romans 5:5 it is written, 'The love of God is shed abroad in our hearts by the Holy Ghost which is given unto us.'

"There are two kinds of love: human love and God's love. Human love fails; God's love never fails. When you are alone with your husband and feel that his depression touches you, pray this prayer: 'Thank you, Lord Jesus, that God's love has been put into my heart through the Holy Spirit who is given to me. Thank you, Father, that your love in me is victorious over this darkness.'"

Later on we met again and she said, "The Lord is working. My husband is so much happier and less depressed. I often repeat the prayer you gave me and I know that if I give room to the Holy Spirit, then I become a channel for His love, which is the fruit of the Holy Spirit. But what can I do when the channel is blocked by my own sins, for often there is self-pity and sometimes bitterness in my heart?"

"Do not try to fight your sins, but obey 1 John 1: 7 and 9. If you confess your sins God will be faithful, true to His promise, and forgive you while the blood of Jesus Christ cleanses from all the sins you confess."

The Bible says, "Live your lives in love—the same sort of love which Christ gives us and which he perfectly expressed when he gave himself up for us" (Eph. 5:2, Phillips). God's love gives us the power to give ourselves up to Him. Love gives vision, and Jesus' paratroopers must have vision to avoid the danger of seeing things out of focus. It is at Golgotha that we are given vision.

> *At the cross, at the cross, where I first saw the light,*
> *And the burden of my heart rolled away,*
> *It was there by faith I received my sight . . .*

God's love is not natural to us nor does it just grow. We are only God's means of demonstrating that love. As our spiritual strength only grows by exercise, so in acting God's love will we become richer. The Holy Spirit will give us His love just when we begin to act it. Like the parachutist after his first descent, when asked what it felt like to launch out, cried out, "It works!", so God's love "works" if we act it out in faith.

Prayer Warriors

Epaphras, another member of your Church, and a real servant of Christ Jesus, sends his greeting. He works hard for you even here, for he prays constantly and earnestly for you.
(Col. 4:12, Phillips)

Two little girls, Betty and Mary, came to speak to me at the close of a meeting in New Zealand. They were very young, yet the smaller of the two asked:

"Do you think I am too young to ask Jesus to come into my heart?"

"Tell me, does your Mama love you?"

"She really does."

"Are you too young for her to love you?"

"Of course not!"

"Do you know that the Lord Jesus loves you far more than your Mama loves you? He said, 'Suffer the little children to come unto me.' I think the Lord Jesus loves children almost more than He loves grown-ups. The Bible says that He is interested even in sparrows, and you are much bigger than a sparrow."

The little girl folded her hands and said, "Lord Jesus, will you come into my heart? I have often been naughty. Will You forgive me?"

I wish you could have seen her happy face!

"And what about you, Mary?"

"I did it three months ago and have prayed for Betty every day since then, and now she has done it."

"Then I think you must pray for a third one, together."

They looked at each other and exclaimed, "Ann."

"Certainly it must be Ann. And after Ann has invited

the Lord Jesus into her heart, you three must pray for a fourth; then the four of you for a fifth, and so on." They promised. The chain reaction of the gospel in the lives of these two little sparrows was due to the power of prayer.

PRAYER BREAKS RESISTANCE

And they overcame him by the blood of the Lamb. (Rev. 12:11)

It was also in Christchurch that I spoke to a group of young people about surrender. Looking around the meeting, I could see two girls were resisting the Holy Spirit as their faces grew harder and harder.

I prayed to the Lord for wisdom and guidance, and in obedience to Him, I paused in my message and said, "Young people, there are two among you who are resisting the Holy Spirit. If they continue in this there is a danger that they will go home poorer than they were when they came. But if they stop resisting they will go home richer. For the Lord has a blessing for them. Let us pray together that the Lord will send away the spirit of disobedience and break their resistance by the Holy Spirit."

I believe that sometimes it is better, even necessary, to take the offensive. We are able to do this knowing that we stand on the victorious side, overcoming by the blood of the Lamb.

After praying I went on with my talk, refraining from looking at the two girls. At the close of the meeting one of them came to me and asked how I had known that she had rejected the Lord. I replied that both her face and the Holy Spirit had shown it very clearly.

She continued, "It is true. I have a boy-friend who is not a Christian and I was so afraid that I would have to give him up that I was not willing to surrender. But now I see that I must."

"Will you pray, 'Lord Jesus, make me willing to be made willing to surrender all'?"

She did; and I saw something of the unspeakable joy, full of glory, on her face. To lose your life for Jesus' sake is to win it; what a joy that is!

Prayer had broken the resistance. As someone has pointed out, the sermon which brought three thousand souls to Christ and from which the missionary movement from Jerusalem was launched began as the irresistible answer to ten days' prayer in that upper room where one hundred and twenty had met.

THE TOP-DRESSER

For we walk by faith, not by sight. (2 Cor. 5:7)

While visiting the mother of one of my friends who had recently suffered a nervous breakdown, her conversation turned constantly to her own depression and suffering. I prayed to the Lord that He would give me the right message to show her God's answer to her problems. What a joy it is to know that the Lord has promised us wisdom when we need it (Jas. 1:5). How I prayed that He would give her that upward look which is so necessary for waking up to reality: seeing the vision of Jesus' victory.

She told me, "I feel that I have committed so many sins that I don't feel that there is any forgiveness for me. When I am reading the Bible, I don't feel that the promises are for me. I feel far from God and so depressed that I cannot do my work."

I noticed that she used the word 'feel' four times. This reminded me of an experience I had when I was in New Zealand working with Dr. Edwin Orr.

I was in a place called Thames giving a series of talks in a campaign, the last meeting of which was to be held that coming Sunday in the big town hall. I like campaigns: though God can do and does great things in a once-for-all, here was the opportunity to give out the gospel message and to explain the victorious life. The final meeting of such a series is often a climax when I can make a challenge for decisions. What a joy it is to see the Holy Spirit working and people answering 'Yes' to Jesus, which makes the angels rejoice.

Such a meeting can be a great strain, so I was looking forward to having a few free days after this one. You can imagine therefore my mixed emotions when Dr. Orr wrote from Dargaville asking me to join him there to continue his campaign for a further week. He had previously planned to finish his meetings on Sunday, as I had done mine, and had already arranged to start another campaign elsewhere on the following day. However, the people of Dargaville had been awakened and wanted to continue. There were signs of revival in the town. So I agreed to go.

All information that I could obtain showed bus connections to be impossible. I understood that the only way to reach Dargaville in time was by car. This prospect did not make me very happy; although the New Zealanders seem to perform miracles with their roads, some are still in very bad condition. To travel for nine hours would be very tiring.

So I spoke to my heavenly Father, "You know, Father, that I am not strong enough to stand a nine-hour car ride and then give a talk immediately in a town where people are expecting great things from the meetings. Won't you grant a miracle and allow me to go by plane? It's the only way of traveling with the least amount of strain." That evening a man asked me if it were true that I was scheduled to speak in Dargaville on the following Monday.

"Yes, that's right."

"How in the world will you reach there in time?"

"I shall go by plane."

"But there is no airline to Dargaville."

"I know, but our problems are the material used by God when He performs miracles. He knows that flying is the only way I can arrive in time without feeling tired."

He smiled and said, "I work for a top-dressing company. My boss is a Christian. He said that if you need it you can have a lift in one of our top-dressing planes."

I whispered, "Thank you, Father."

"But," he continued, "if the weather is too bad we shall not be able to help you because our planes are not equipped with radar: landing is too dangerous without it in bad weather. On the other hand, if the weather is too good, we shall not be able to help you either for there will be too much top-dressing to do." Top-dressing, I learned, means broadcasting fertilizer over the fields from an airplane.

I invited my friends to pray for weather that would be neither too good nor too bad. I was informed on the day of my departure that there was still some top-dressing to be done in the neighborhood of Dargaville, so even good weather would allow my departure. My informant told me also that they were all praying that I would be a blessing to the pilot, who was a backslider. They hoped the Lord would give me an opportunity to chat to him during the flight. Thanking him for being so helpful, I prepared to leave.

Although I had often traveled by air, this was to be my first trip in a monoplane, and a very small one at that. The first thing the pilot did was to put plugs in his ears. I prayed, "Lord, so often when I want to talk about You people stop their ears." I began to talk to the pilot very softly. . . .

"I cannot understand you," he said.

I spoke even more softly. Then he took the plugs from his ears and asked me to repeat what I had said.

"I only asked why you put those things in your ears."

"Because of the noise of the engine."

And so the conversation started. I knew that people were praying, and God made it a useful talk. The pilot began telling me about the "Whys" in his life. Why had God allowed his young wife to die, leaving him with four small children?

"I can't believe in a God of love who allows such tragedies. I have put aside all religion since her death."

Then I told him about the "Whys" in my own life. Why did my aged father have to die alone in a prison cell when all his children were in the same building? Why did my sister, after ten months of terrible suffering in prison, have to die only one week before I was set free?

"But here," I said, "in this book, the Bible, I can see God's side of the embroidery of our lives. In it God's viewpoint can be seen, and we can learn to get a bird's-eye view of our experiences."

I showed him several texts from the Bible in my hand to illustrate this:

And we know that all things work together for good to
them that love God. (Rom. 8:28)

For I reckon that the sufferings of this present time are
not worthy to be compared with the glory which shall be
revealed in us. (Rom. 8:18)

It was a good thing that he could not avoid me, so I was
able to show him many other portions of scripture!

At last he spoke, "You know, Miss ten Boom, all the things
you say sound very nice, but I don't feel that they are true.
But, I must interrupt our talk. I must warn you that we are
flying into cloud. For the first ten minutes you will have the
feeling that we are leaning too much to one side. Don't be
afraid because I'm piloting on my instruments and the plane
will be kept absolutely straight."

"That is the best illustration I have ever heard," I told
him. "It is not safe to pilot on feelings. My Bible is my in-
strument; flying on the Bible's instructions, acting on its read-
ings, my plane keeps a straight course. If I pilot on my feelings, I could make dangerous mistakes."

I am glad to report that the pilot said a new "Yes" to Jesus.
Paul explains the reason of this conflict between feelings and
fact in First Corinthians 1 and 2. The realm of the wisdom of
the wise is in conflict with the kingdom of God's foolishness.
Man's wisdom is found by sense-knowledge—feeling, seeing,
reasoning—but faith-knowledge is in the greater dimension
of God's foolishness which is the highest wisdom.

Don't try to bring down the foolishness of faith into the
realm of sense-knowledge. Rather allow the Holy Spirit to
teach you to lift up the wisdom of your wise-ness to the
plane of faith-knowledge. Then you will see and feel from
God's point of view.

PREACHING WOMEN

"The Lord gives the word of power; the women who bear and publish (the news) are a great host." (Psa. 68:11, Amp.)

I am sometimes asked if I ever encounter the difficulties involved when people show their dislike of women speaking in public. My answer is that I do not experience such problems because I will not go where they do not allow me to speak!

On one such occasion, in New Zealand, I received a letter from some people inviting me to speak in a certain town. They wrote: "You understand that you may not teach us. You can give your testimony, but be scriptural and obey 1 Cor. 14:34–35."

I replied, "If by this you mean that I must come with a closed Bible, then I cannot accept your invitation. I am always happy to give my testimony to glorify the Lord, but only to underline the gospel. I come to teach the Word of God, not 'to talk about my own experiences.'"

Immediately an answer came, "Forget what we have written. We have heard that God is blessing the meetings where you speak."

Later, after my arrival in that town, we discussed this question.

"But do you not, yourself, have the feeling that you are disobedient?" they questioned me anxiously. "Paul says in both First Timothy 2:11–12 and First Corinthians 14:34–35 that women must be silent."

"Yes, that is so; but we must understand what the words mean and do not mean, and how they apply to this day and age. Peter gave us a picture of the present age in the words of

Joel when he quoted, 'I will pour out of my Spirit upon all flesh: and your sons and your daughters shall prophesy.' Now what is prophecy? First Corinthians says it is edification, exhortation, and comfort."

"But surely Peter meant that these things happened at the first Pentecost."

"Yes, it partly happened then, 'these things' they were witnessing. But in the full quotation, Peter proceeded to things which did not take place then: 'Blood, and fire, and vapor of smoke,' have not yet come to pass, nor yet 'The sun shall be turned into darkness, and the moon into blood' (see Acts 2:16–21)." We know from other scriptures that these things will happen before the return of the Lord Jesus (Matt. 24:29 and Rev. 6:12).

We live in the days past the beginning of prophecy and before the end of it. God says, "And on my male and female slaves [literal translation] I will pour out in those days of my Spirit; and they shall prophesy." There is no distinction of race in this verse. The power is to any devoted servant of Christ, Jew or Gentile, male or female. The one hundred and twenty at the first Pentecost included certain women; all were filled with the Spirit, all spoke languages they had never learned (Acts 2:4–11).

"While in First Corinthians 11:5 we find that women prophesied in the assembly, it is not that Paul is forbidding but merely regulating it by the covering of the head. This verse also says that women prayed in church. Again in Acts 21:9 it is mentioned that Philip's four daughters prophesied, not because prophesying by women was rare, but because it was unusual for four women of one family to do so."

"But First Corinthians 14:34–35 clearly states that

women must be silent in the church," they insisted.

"I believe this must be interpreted in the light of these other scriptures and should not conflict with them. I am sure that it means that women should be silent when someone else is speaking ('let them ask their own husbands at home'). Miriam, Deborah, Anna—they are all good company for me. We are all given encouragement in Psalm 68:11 where the Revised Version says, 'The women that publish the tidings are a great host.'

"Over and above all this there is one thing to which neither man nor woman dare turn a blind eye: the anointing of the Holy Spirit which alone fits them to speak for God (Acts 2:18)."

How can I disobey His direct command, to lift up my eyes and look on the fields? Truly they are white to harvest. Thus I sought to meet their legal objections.

Seven

Outreach to the Outback

Who are you to criticize the servant of somebody else, especially when that somebody else is God? (Rom. 14:4, Phillips)

Farms in Australia often show the signs of pioneering life. There is plenty of land so that farmers think in huge numbers: one thousand acres or twenty thousand sheep. Many of the houses appear to have been hurriedly put together, and there is much evidence of damage by white ants or termites, little creatures, but dangerous—like little sins.

The problem of dealing with them has been solved in Australia through the use of a poison which exterminates them. As soon as they are discovered (usually underneath the house where the queen termite has made her nest) the exterminator uses his poison on a number of ants. When these die they become tasty morsels for other ants who in turn are poisoned. This goes on until the poison reaches the queen. She dies and it is but a short time before all the termites are dead.

My host, Ted, and his sister are Swedish settlers. It was a joy to be in the company of this family and to share Christian fellowship with them, for they love the Lord and study His Word, of which they have a great knowledge. They also have a deep burden for souls. While I was with Ted and his sister, I accompanied them on several visits to friends and acquaintances.

One day we took a long trip in their car and came to a point where the car could go no further. We had to halt at the thick bush, just like a jungle, and were forced to get out and walk. We pushed our way through until suddenly we were in a garden of beautiful flowers. Birds sang; it was a paradise in the midst of the wood.

At the door of a little house in the clearing stood a poorly dressed woman who invited us to enter. We went inside a room so dirty, so full of junk that there was scarcely a place to sit down. But we had a fruitful talk.

Although they lived so far away in this lonely spot in a filthy house surrounded by a garden paradise, both the women and her son were wide open to listen to the message of the gospel. Both took that first important step of inviting Jesus to come into their hearts. Ted promised that he would do the "follow-up" work and visit them regularly to help them with Bible study.

After a long return walk and tiring ride in the car, Ted asked me to make another visit with him. This time it was not to take the gospel but to meet one of the saints of the village, an elderly woman shut in by sickness. She was a pillar of the little church.

We had just an hour in which to enjoy fellowship, and I was looking forward to meeting her, hoping that each of us would be "helped by the other's faith," as Paul says in Romans 1:12 (Phillips).

What a disappointment was mine! The conversation turned to some terrible things a liberal theologian had said about the Bible. Ted himself is a "fighting fundamentalist" and could add many other examples.

At the end of an hour I was shocked to silence; in all my tours of Australia and New Zealand, I had never heard such stories of Bible criticism.

Back in the car Ted asked me what I thought of the visit.

"I am so sorry that our time has been wasted," I answered. "We have not had a moment to pray or read the Scriptures nor even to share with each other one happy experience in the Lord—and all three of us have undoubtedly known Him. The whole time has been used to complain about someone else's sin and theological weakness.

"Do you think that the Lord was in our conversation? Ted, we need to pray that the Holy Spirit will give us sound theology and the discernment of the spirits which we need very much, for we live in an age when, 'if it were possible, they shall deceive even the very elect' (Matt. 24:24). On the other hand, we must watch that the enemy does not push us into wasting our time by talking about the theological sins of others.

"Paul says in Romans 14 'After all, who are you to criticize the servant of somebody else, especially when that somebody else is God? It is to his own master that he gives, or fails to give, satisfactory service. And don't doubt that satisfaction, for God is well able to transform men into servants who are satisfactory.' Let us redeem the time, because the days are evil (Eph. 5:16)."

The following morning in the barn where the cows were being milked I overheard a conversation: Ted was telling his mother about the talk he had had with me.

"Mother, I'll never again use my time for such useless

stuff as criticism."

I was able to say a "Thank you" to the Lord as the Holy Spirit revived true life. For when we see our sins and failures we forget those of others, and the Lord can bless.

ANOTHER WASTED HOUR

Be wise in your behavior toward non-Christians, and make the best possible use of your time. (Col. 4:5, Phillips)

During my visit to Australia a good-looking Dutchman came to me, telling his name. Very surprised I asked, "Are you Steventje's son?"

"I am."

When I was young my mother always had a helper in the kitchen, and I have the sweetest memories of all the different servants who shared our home life and were always accepted as members of our family.

This young man's mother had been one of them, becoming a very great friend of ours; so when she married she kept in touch with us. I had heard that one of her sons had left home, more or less the black sheep. What a joy that God had given the opportunity of meeting him. How I wished I could bring him to the Lord.

"We must spend some more time together. As I have a free evening, will you come and tell me all the news of your mother . . . and bring your photographs!" So it was agreed and Jack arrived at the appointed time.

I had a whole evening to look at his photographs and gather news of his family. During this I was much in prayer that I should be shown the best opportunity in which to start speaking about his soul. My host and I had also prayed for him earlier in the day.

I was very careful: Dutch people do not like to be "button-holed." I asked him about his wife; she was a barmaid but a decent one. I warned him that the people she served would not always be very good and decent.

When more than an hour had passed chatting like this I gathered my courage and said, "Jack, your parents are faithful Christians. What about you? Do you serve the Lord?"

"No, I don't."

"Do you realize that your soul is very precious in God's eyes and that there is only one step necessary to enter the kingdom of God—that of receiving the Lord Jesus? He died for you and suffered your punishment. Bring your sins to Him and trust Him as your Savior. He is such a wonderful Friend."

"I will."

We prayed; Jack's face was very happy after he had made that great decision. I showed him the next steps: how, by being born into God's family, the Bible's promises are ours. God opens wide the doors of His house of plenty and bids us come and take with boldness.

"Jack, when you came this evening to see me, what were you thinking?" I was curious to know as he had found the Lord so simply.

"I was praying the whole way along, 'God, please make her bring me to You.'"

And here I had been, marking time, anxiously awaiting the right moment! Yet all the time there had been a hungry heart longing for salvation. A wasted hour!

The following evening Jack returned with his wife. I asked her if she would trust Jesus as her Savior, but her reply was joyous, "I have. Jack brought me to Him today and I am so very, very happy."

Dr. J. H. Jowett once wrote:

> There are times that we need a "tonic" in order that our poor ministries may be converted into powerful weapons. And, blessed be God, we have the promise of this redemptive work in the very measure in which the Holy Spirit is revealed to us. He is called the Renewer, the Reviver, the Restorer of souls, and by His baptism, the poorest, weakest agent can be turned into a powerful soul-winner.

ROCK AND ROLL

I am the good shepherd, and I know those that are mine and my sheep know me. (John 10:14, Phillips)

The Lord has taught me that I can pray and preach at the same time—a vertical and horizontal connection. What I say to my heavenly Father is quite different to what I am telling the people in front of me.

If, for example, some fall asleep, I pray that first God will awaken me for I am guilty of giving a drowsy speech. Then I ask the Lord to awaken them. When they open their eyes I add, "Keep them awake, Lord," and finally, as they begin to listen, I ask a double blessing for them.

It is not only for sleepy people that I pray! Often I can read on the faces of others that there is a battle going on within their hearts and I must wrestle in prayer for victory.

At a meeting in Australia, my talk was primarily for Christians. However, I have learned to take no congregation for granted, so I first explained the way of salvation. The Lord led me to call for a moment of silence to give those who desired an opportunity to accept Jesus. After that I said that all who had said a real "Yes" to the Lord were invited to enter right into the treasure-house of God's plenty and take with boldness the promises given in the Bible.

After the meeting I found six boys in the inquiry room. One of them was a boy with a rugged face and one arm in plaster whom I had noticed earlier in the evening.

I said to one of the others, "Did you ever receive Jesus as your Savior?"

His answer was surprising: "Yes," he said; "At the beginning of your talk, all five of us did. During the whole meeting we have been praying for Jim, here. Please bring him to the Lord." He pointed to the lad with the broken arm.

"That will not be difficult. The Lord put it into my heart to pray for him too." Indeed, it was not difficult, for the ground of his heart had been prepared by prayer. Jim asked the Lord to forgive his sins and to enter his heart. At the end of our talk together he said:

"I have a problem and wonder if you can help me?"

"Tell me what it is. Maybe I can."

"You know I . . . I am terribly fond of rock and roll."

That was a problem! How could I help him? I am so thankful for the promise in James 1:5 (Phillips): "If, in the process, any of you does not know how to meet any particular problem he has only to ask God—who gives generously to all men without making them feel foolish or guilty—and he may be quite sure that the necessary wisdom will be given him." I cashed that check, written in the name of every member of God's family—the Lord even gave a bit of humor to start!

"Jim, you now belong to Jesus, and Jesus belongs to you.

Now you are standing on the solid Rock, Jesus Christ, and you are on the roll of heaven. That is now your 'Rock and roll'!"

I understood that this did not solve the problem, and so I advised, "You are not alone any more. The Lord Jesus is your great Friend. When you go to a dance, do not forget that He is with you; and if He should say, 'Jim, I really cannot go to that place,' then do not go by yourself without Him."

Jim promised.

I do not believe in immediately telling new Christians what they should and should not do: such things can be left safely to the Holy Spirit. For, after all, we do not bring people to a faith, a religion or a doctrine, but to a person, Jesus Christ.

Oswald Chambers, in his *Workmen of God*, illustrates the power of Christ and his Holy Spirit to cause people to follow Him wholly and to burn their past as they begin to shine for Him. As the arctic temperatures keep a thermometer frozen until there are warmer conditions and then the mercury registers, so we are "frozen toward God" until we come in contact with Jesus Christ. Then we thaw out and our lives register and tell out for the Lord. The Holy Spirit will make men alive unto God.

All new Christians are like Jim, but I pray that God will make them warm and then they will obey the Holy Spirit and not even want their old ways of living.

A FATHER WITH TWO LITTLE BOYS

You must let little children come to me,
and you must never stop them. (Matt. 19:14, Phillips)

Praise the Lord for the Navigators! Their counselors' training and Scripture-memorizing courses have done more good in follow-up work for "babes" in Christ all over the world than anything else I know.

What a joy it is, after a strenuous meeting, to find the counselors in the inquiry room, well equipped with literature and practical knowledge of Bible verses as well as trained in methods of approaching the enquirers. They have also been taught to maintain contact by telephone, letter or visits in the weeks following the initial counseling. In places where counselors are not prepared for campaigns, I miss them badly.

In a big church in Australia, I saw a little boy raise his hand when I gave the invitation for those people who wanted to make a decision for Christ. Toward the end of the meeting I said, "I wonder if the father of the little boy who raised his hand would be so kind as to go with him to the inquiry room."

Immediately the father stood up and took not only one but two little boys by the hand into the room behind the platform. I saw there were no counselors. Why did the minister not go?

I finished the meeting and quickly joined these three. I will never forget the scene there. The father was on his knees, an arm round each kneeling child, all three crying with emotion. Indeed, I could not keep back my own tears as I knelt with them, listening as the father, with great tenderness, led his own sons to the Lord.

Afterward I asked him if he would come back for the rest of the week to assist me in the counseling. Though no one else came to help, there was great blessing in the inquiry room that week.

NAVIGATORS

You hold in your hands the very word of life.
(Phil. 2:16, Phillips)

With a kangaroo hop back to New Zealand for a return visit of two months before setting out for India, I was able to meet again many for whom I was used of the Lord to bring to a trust in Him for salvation. They were faithfully studying the Navigators' course in memorizing Scripture. Rarely am I able to visit a country so soon (often it is five years) so what a delight to find the recently converted Christians profiting from this course, and not only they but some of the older ones whom they had interested.

Every member of one family in Hamilton was faithfully studying the correspondence course, even Grandma. When the lessons were returned, the youngest girl would ask, "Grandma, how many mistakes did you make? I only made two!" Seldom have I seen a family where every member had such a practical knowledge of the Scriptures.

I decided that since I know fewer Scriptures by heart in English than I do in Dutch, I would study the course myself. My trip to Korea interrupted these lessons as I had two hundred and fifty meetings in three months. I had to discontinue learning, but I hope to start again as soon as I have a little more time.

It is good to be certain why we find power in the Word of God. Here are five reasons why I believe the Bible is inspired:

1. It says so! "Holy men of God spake as they were moved by the Holy Ghost." (2 Pet. 1:21)

2. The effect it has upon all who believe and follow it.
3. Though some of it was written more than two thousand years before the letters of the New Testament, yet the writers agree.
4. The authors do not offer any excuses for their own faults or sins.
5. The writers record some most harrowing scenes which affected them greatly, yet they never express one word of emotion. The Holy Spirit wanted the facts recorded and not their feelings about the facts.

Many persons make the mistake of thinking that they can measure the certainty of their salvation by their feelings. It is the Word of God that is their foundation, and therefore it is essential for the new convert in Christ to have a practical knowledge of the Bible.

More than anyone else it is the new convert who will come under the fire of the enemy. He needs knowledge of the Sword of the Spirit. As the Lord Jesus used this Sword to overcome the evil one in temptation, so he must learn to defend himself against every sort of attack.

One of his favorite darts fired at the new convert is "It is not true that you are really saved." This must be met with Scripture such as this in 1 John 5:11–12: "And this is the record, that God hath given us eternal life, and this life is in his Son. He that hath the Son hath life; and he that hath not the Son of God hath not life."

Another form of attack that Satan uses is to bring to the memory of the young convert the weaknesses and sins of the past and then suggest that because of them he can never be called a faithful follower of Christ. No amount of reasoning or argument can overcome this temptation but only the Word of God. It says in First Corinthians 10:13, "There hath no temptation taken you but such as is common to man: but God is faithful, who will not suffer you to be tempted above that ye are able; but will with the temptation also make a way of escape, that ye may be able to bear it."

The third attack is one that tries to rob the young Christian of his assurance of forgiveness. The Bible answers this in first John 1:9, where we read, "If we confess our sins, he is faithful and just to forgive us our sins, and to cleanse us from all unrighteousness." Here God not only promises to forgive us but also to cleanse us. What a gracious provision! The spirit of worry can weaken courage, and so we need to know John 16:24: "Hitherto have ye asked nothing in my name; ask, and ye shall receive, that your joy may be full."

The Word of God is like a checkbook with all the promises made out in our names and signed by Jesus Christ at the very moment we are born again into the family of God. How can young converts learn to cash their checks? In the first place they must know the promises.

To obtain the Scripture memorizing and Bible study courses, contact:

NavPress
P.O. Box 35002
Colorado Springs, CO 80935
1-800-366-7788
www.navpress.com

Eight

Random Reflections

Restore unto me the joy of thy salvation. (Ps. 51:12)

In an American university, I spoke with a girl whose problem was temptations. "I doubt," she said, "whether I am a Christian. I did make a decision for Christ and trusted Him as my Savior but I am so often filled with temptations—terrible thoughts enter into my head and my heart—that I fear I am not a Christian at all."

"Temptation is no sin," I replied. "Jesus was tempted. As a great preacher once said, 'You cannot stop birds from flying over your head, but you can prevent them from building a nest in your hair.' The Lord Jesus gives the strength needed in order that we may not yield to temptation. What about your parents? Are you still their daughter, even when you sin?"

"Yes, I am: but a naughty one."

"That is so. A sinning child of God is still a child of God, but a disobedient one."

"But I have lost my joy."

"That is because sin causes us to lose our fellowship. Your relationship with Him is just the same. Jesus will be your Victor. He died for you and now He lives for you."

Living, He loved me; Dying, He saved me;
Buried, He carried my sins far away;
Rising, He justified freely forever;
One day He's coming—oh, glorious day!

•   •   •

We are in training for that great future, but this training period can be a victorious one only when we realize that we can and must surrender ourselves to the Lord Jesus.

Live as rich as you are; cash your checks in the Bible; realize that you are what you are in Jesus Christ. The devil says that the bank account of the Bible is frozen by your sins. He is a liar. That bank account is full of the precious reserves of heaven's plenty.

Surrender your past, present and future. Your past is a canceled check; your present is cash; your future is a promissory note. Jesus bore your sins on the cross; all was done and finished at Calvary. Now He lives for us.

When we forgive others, we "bury the hatchet"; but sometimes we leave the handle out, ready for future use. God does not. He blots out our sins like a cloud. You never see a cloud again once it has evaporated.

We are on the Lord's side and thus are yoke-fellows with Jesus, so we can face the foe, being more than conquerors through Him who loves us. Do not ask, "Can I be kept from sinning if I keep close to Him?" But rather, "Can I be kept from sinning if He keeps close to me?"

You will see what a joy it is to surrender to Jesus. He will go with you to the point where you went astray and change the whole situation with His presence.

Hallelujah! What a Savior!

"Falling in the water does not drown you—but staying in it." (Bob Doing)

COCKTAIL PARTIES

Cast thy bread upon the waters: for thou shalt find it after many days. (Eccles. 11:1)

When Spurgeon was once asked if the heathen who had never heard the gospel would be saved, his reply is reputed to be, "Will you be saved when you do not bring them the gospel?" What a responsibility we have to every creature in every place, even the unexpected place.

In Savannah, Georgia, I was invited to a dinner party. After driving to the coast, I was welcomed in a beautiful house with a terrace near the sea. An abundance of flowers and shrubs made a paradise of the garden, and over the water the sun was setting, turning the sky into a symphony of color. Servants offered drinks and sweets; people were friendly; I was enjoying the evening immensely.

A rich dinner of the most delicious foods was served later on, which I much appreciated as it was not long since I had been in a concentration camp. However, I was sorry to see how much people were drinking throughout the evening. For my own part, I was able to quench my thirst and remain perfectly sober with a supply of soft drinks.

After dining everyone gathered in a beautiful lounge where I was to give a talk. One man who had taken too many cocktails was asleep, but most of the company were sober. (It amazes me how many drinks some people can take without becoming drunk.) I prayed for great wisdom.

Deep down I was not happy about this gathering. I have witnessed a great deal of poverty, and it hurt my heart to see so much spent on personal satisfaction. Yet the Lord had shown me that I must use every opportunity to give the gospel; these people were included—all with souls to lose or gain for eternity. I was there and knew the way to heaven, having in my handbag a Bible, that Book which tells us that Jesus loves sinners and wants to make them children of God. "Whosoever believeth in him should not perish, but have everlasting life" (John 3:16).

I began by speaking about my war experiences: how, standing in front of the crematorium where eighty per cent of the prisoners were cremated, I had woken up to reality. I told them of the joy that was mine because I knew I had everlasting life through the Lord Jesus Christ in whom I trusted.

"We are not in a concentration camp here," I continued, "but to everyone present comes that moment of facing eternity. Are you right with God? Do you know that here and now Jesus can bring you into contact with the ocean of God's love? Come to Him; repent; bring your sins to Him. He will save you."

I did not give this message in sermon form but wove it into my stories. All but the one man, who was fast asleep and loudly snoring, listened attentively. I think that for most of them it was the first time that they had heard the gospel.

Afterward a lady asked, "Tomorrow I am giving a cocktail party in my home. Will you come and give a talk there too?"

So for five evenings of that one week I gave talks at various cocktail parties. Later I had to go on a diet—there was far too much "Corrie ten Boom" after so many lovely dinners. But oh, the joy of being given the opportunity to reach so many lost sheep!

Does the seed sown in such strange surroundings sprout? Two years later I met again one of the ladies whom I had seen at those parties. She was in great trouble and I had the lovely privilege then to be used by the Lord to bring her to repentance, to see her come from darkness into the light of salvation in Jesus Christ. As Sam Shoemaker so rightly put it:

> It should be the most natural thing in the world for us to lead people to the turning point of their lives. If we have traveled this road ourselves, we know its turnings and its straitways, its high places and its low. If a man asks you the way to a turn and you know it, it is not presumptuous or in any way unnatural to show him the right direction. When human spirits are looking for the heavenly city, for someone who knows the way it is quite natural to say, "I have been where you are. I hardly knew what I was looking for, but another took me by the hand and showed me the way. As far as I traveled, it has been a good way. Will you join me and let us travel together?"

REJOICING ANGELS AT A DINNER PARTY

The solid fact is Christ. (Col. 2:17, Phillips)

While I was in Japan, there was a large section of the American army still stationed in Yokohama. Here I was invited to a dinner given by Mrs. Clark, an officer's wife, whom I had met at the church ladies' meeting. Several officers and their wives were invited, some being keen Christians, and it was one of these who drove me to the party. We prayed in the car that the Lord would make us a blessing.

After the meal we had a lively conversation; but suddenly my hostess made a remark which, although I have forgotten, was so strange that I answered, "How can you, a Christian, say that?" One of the officers added:

"But do you know that she is a Christian? Isn't there a condition to fulfill, a personal decision for the Lord Jesus to be made, in order that one may enter into the family of God?"

I had really taken it for granted that she had made her decision, for I had met her in church meetings. But I took that opportunity to ask her if she had ever received Jesus as her Savior.

"I never have," was the reply. "How in the world do I do that?"

This was my opportunity to tell her, but can the way of salvation be shown in such company? Would she not be embarrassed? Fortunately the other Christians present at that party were a real team, for suddenly the room was full of conversation as they all started to talk together.

In our corner my hostess and I were able to talk as though we were the only people in the room. I showed her that salvation is a gift and that, as a gift, it can only be received by one who is willing to accept such bounty.

"You know that you are a sinner? Bring your sins to Him; then receive His forgiveness and salvation. Receiving Jesus gives you power, 'power to become the sons of God' (John 1:12). Thus you must first repent of your sins. We will pray together; there is no need to shut your eyes; nobody will see what we are doing."

We both prayed, and she told the Lord of her decision, the decision that always makes the angels rejoice. As suddenly as it started, the conversation just as suddenly stopped;

and in the quiet of that moment she said:

"I have just received the Lord Jesus as my Savior. I trust Him to have made me a child of God." Her husband made a cynical remark, but she replied, "Don't say such a thing. I meant it and I know that I am now a Christian."

In the car going home the officer, who had been such a willing chauffeur, suggested prayer; together we thanked the Lord for what He had done at the dinner party.

Five years later I met a young Japanese woman who was on fire for the Lord, telling people of the gospel wherever she could. "It was Mrs. Clark who brought me to the Lord," she told me. While today in America there is a family in which everyone works together in Sunday School and mid-week meetings, spreading the gospel. It is the family of Mrs. Clark, the officer's wife who found the Lord Jesus during a dinner party in her own home in Japan.

MUST ONE KNOW ONE'S SPIRITUAL BIRTHDAY?

I often think of that genuine faith of yours—a faith that first appeared in your grandmother Lois, then in Eunice your mother, and is now, I am convinced, in you as well.
(2 Tim. 1:5, Phillips)

Once I was asked by a girl in America, "Corrie, when were you born again?"

I don't know. I am like the man who was asked when he was born. His reply was that he did not know when he was born; he just knew that he was born! I think that I must have been born again when I was very young, for at the age of five the Lord made me into a real intercessor, leading me to pray for the people in a street behind our block.

In this street there were many wine merchants and a great deal of drunkenness. It was because of this that I was so burdened for their salvation. "Lord, save all the people in the Smedestraat" was my repeated prayer. God honors prayer, including those of little children.

When I was about twenty, I worked in a Christian Girl Guide camp. One evening after I had brought the gospel to about eighteen girls, seated around our camp fire, we talked over the message in the big tent before we went to bed. One of the girls said, "Do you know that we are neighbors of a kind? I have always lived in the Smedestraat."

"I lived there too," another girl remarked.

"My parents' home was there," added a third.

It appeared that all the girls or their families had lived there at some time. Suddenly I saw God's pattern. As a child I had naively prayed for a whole street; now at twenty years of age, God gave me the opportunity to bring the message of salvation to the very people for whom I had had a burden.

There is no set pattern of how to be saved. But one must have assurance of salvation. If that is not present, a clear-cut decision has to be made. Jesus wants our hearts. There can be nothing vague or uncertain in our relationship with Him.

"I know whom I have believed, and am persuaded that he is able to keep that which I have committed unto him against that day" (2 Tim. 1:12).

CANOE RIDE ON A JUNGLE RIVER

*Behold, now is the accepted time; behold, now is
the day of salvation.* (2 Cor. 6:2)

In the state of Kerala in India, I was enjoying one of the most peaceful journeys I have ever experienced: traveling in a small canoe down a river in the jungle. Slowly our little craft glided over the shallow waters. Except for the rhythmic sound of the paddle and the occasional murmur of the soft wind in the trees, there was nothing to be heard.

My companion and I were on our way to a conference. He was one of the Indians who use their homes for prayer groups where they plead for revival. Twice a year all the groups come together for Bible study and prayer.

It was at several such conferences that I had been invited to speak three times a day. The people gather in a *pandal* (a wide roof protecting the congregation from the hot sun) with the grassy floor providing the seats and no walls to allow as much air through as possible in the hot sticky atmosphere.

While the coolie was paddling our canoe through the water, the Indian brother and I had plenty of time for talking. He told me of the great longing in his heart to win souls for Jesus Christ.

"I feel," he said, "that I have not been successful. I always give my testimony, but I do not manage to persuade people to make a decision for Christ."

"Do you use the Sword of the Spirit, the Word of God?"

"I fear I am not very adept at handling that Sword. At the critical moment I can never find a text that fits the situation."

I can understand that! I had to learn to overcome this problem also. It is possible to know quite a lot of the Bible and yet not know where to find apt texts. I shared with my companion some of the texts I sometimes use, but reminded him that these are only 'First Aid' verses. It is the Holy Spirit who is willing to give us the right words and Scripture references. If we depend on Him, we are like branches of the vine which bear fruit but from which no fruit can ever grow if they are detached or broken off from the vine.

I often start with Isaiah 53:6: "All we like sheep have gone astray; we have turned every one to his own way." I ask the inquirer, "Which way have you been going until now?" Most of them answer that they have gone their own way, although they add that they have tried to go God's way. Isaiah says we have gone our own way.

It is a good thing for us to realize that this applies to each of us individually; for there is one kind of person Jesus would not and could not help: the Pharisees. They insisted that they walked in God's law and followed His ways. But to those who come to Jesus knowing that they need salvation, Christ says in Matthew 11:28, "Come unto me, all ye that labor and are heavy laden, and I will give you rest." "I came not to call the righteous, but sinners to repentance" (Luke 5:32).

Now reading further in Isaiah 5 we find, "The Lord hath laid on him the iniquity of us all." God has laid on Jesus the sins of us all, and to illustrate this I transfer my Bible from my right hand to my left. In the same way that I place my Bible onto my left hand, so too God laid upon Jesus our sins when He died on the cross.

It was at the cross that everything was done which had to be done. From us Jesus only expects acceptance. John 1:12 reads: "As many as received him. . . ." He loves us and wants our hearts. Just as a young man asks a girl to accept him, so Christ expects a clear-cut decision which the Bible expresses in another place as coming out of darkness into His light.

If, in the margin of your Bible, you write "John 1:12" by

Isaiah 53:6 and in the margin by the verse in John 1 you write "Revelation 3:20," you will very easily be able to see the next step.

So often people ask what they have to do to accept Jesus. The words of Revelation 3:20 make it so clear: "Behold, I stand at the door, and knock," says Jesus, "if any man hear my voice, and open the door, I will come in to him." This is something a child can understand. Jesus does not force the door. I once heard someone say, "The Lord Jesus is a perfect Gentleman; He knocks and waits until we open."

We must be careful not to give too many texts at the beginning, for that can be embarrassing. The most important one at this stage is 1 John 1:7 and 9—confess, repent and be cleansed.

However, first we must give the inquirer time to pray so that he can ask Jesus to come into his heart. When he is praying we can hear whether he has understood! If he says, "Make me good, Lord," or "Teach me to have a good prayer life," then tactfully point out that Jesus will do this and other things after He has been received into the inquirer's heart. Remind him that a lawyer is willing to do business only after he has been accepted as the advocate.

We can trust the Holy Spirit to give the person the right words. Often I myself pray first, asking the Lord to open the way between God and the inquirer and to drive away the "Yes, buts," the doubts which the enemy throws between.

It is such a joy to know that we do not work alone but that it is the Holy Spirit who works with us as His tools. That is why it is so important to pray before, during and after the conversation.

As our canoe continued its journey down the river, my

Indian companion responded thoughtfully, "I see. But how can you have a horizontal and vertical connection at the same time—praying and speaking together?"

"It is a question of practice."

"What texts can I use then?"

"Romans 10:10 shows us that believing and confessing go hand in hand. 1 John 5:13 gives the solid assurance of knowing that we have eternal life in Jesus Christ. Romans 6:23 shows the contrast between the wages of sin, which is death, and the gift of God through Jesus Christ which is life.

"Finally, I ask the inquirer, 'What does the Bible say you are now?' Then I show him John 1:12. The answer then is, 'I am a child of God.' To which I reply, 'Do you feel that?' Sometimes the answer is 'Yes'; then I show that although he can thank God for this feeling, the basis of the assurance is the Word of God so that when our feelings fail us we can still trust the Word. After a while you will find your own choice of texts but you can certainly start with the ones I have mentioned."

I prayed with my Indian brother that God would make him a wide-open channel for His streams of living waters.

By this time the forest had thinned out on either side of the river. We could see narrow paths which permitted the people to tread single file through the trees. On one bank the woods ended abruptly. It was now dark, and I saw, coming along the country roads, little files of Indians, lighting their paths by torches of palm leaves in their hands. The white clothes they wore gave the scene a strangely ethereal apearance as though they were pilgrims walking to heaven.

Those already gathered in the *pandal* away in the distance were singing a Christian song in unison, repeating it many times while the white-robed pilgrims with their flickering torches picked up the refrain. I thought of Psalm 30:4: "Sing unto the Lord, O ye saints of his." It was a foresaste of that time when "the earth shall be full of the knowledge of the Lord, as the waters cover the sea" (Isa. 11:9).

Nine

European Etches

That . . . intercessions . . . be made. (1 Tim. 2:1)

In England two ladies came to me after a meeting. They were neighbors, and one had been praying for the other for several weeks. It was easy to see that the other needed prayer for her eyes were sad. So I prayed with them that God would give us a profitable talk with understanding on both sides. Then I asked her, "Have you ever received Jesus as your Savior?"

"No, I haven't, but I should like to."

I showed her how Jesus in His great love asks us to make a decision to trust Him. He holds out to us the great gift of salvation, but we must be willing to stretch out our hands to take it.

"I wish I could . . ." she replied wistfully.

"Why not?"

"I don't know . . . but really my heart longs to have peace. I know Jesus is willing and able to give me peace and salvation, but it is as if something is holding me back. I have often heard the gospel, but yet I cannot take the step."

I was thoughtful for a moment, praying for guidance. Then I asked, "When did you go to a fortune-teller?"

Looking a little surprised she told me that she had been to one the year before. "But what has that to do with the things we are talking about now? I did it for fun and don't really believe in fortune-tellers."

"Do you realize that you have sinned in God's eyes? Yes, a great sin. God calls this an abomination; and that is the reason you cannot accept the Lord." I opened my Bible and read Deuteronomy 18:10–13:

> There shall not be found among you anyone that useth divination, or an observer of times, or an enchanter, or a witch, or a charmer, or a consulter with familiar spirits, or a wizard, or a necromancer. For all that do these things are an abomination unto the Lord: and because of these abominations the Lord thy God doth drive them out from before thee. Thou shalt be perfect with the Lord thy God.

I told her, "These things are an abomination in God's eyes, and if we have anything to do with them, it means we are seeking help from the enemy instead of from God. 'Thou shalt be perfect with the Lord thy God.'"

"I did not know this was a sin but I see it now."

"I am glad you do. Now listen to what the Bible says in 1 John 1:7 and 9. It tells us to confess and be cleansed. The blood of Jesus cleanses you from all the sins you confess."

I prayed with her and thanked God for His warning and forgiveness shown in His Word; and she did what I told her to do. Her prayer was like the cry of one longing to be saved. "Oh Lord, forgive me for this sin in Jesus' name. I did not know it was such a great sin. I thought it was only foolishness but I see now. Forgive me and make me free."

Again I showed her the way of salvation, and without any hesitation she said, "Lord Jesus, I receive you as my Savior."

On the following day I was told the subsequent events by her neighbor. When her friend arrived home, she told her husband that the Lord Jesus had made her a child of God. He was not at all pleased.

"I don't like this business of conversion and being saved. You have always been a member of the church and a good woman." And becoming very excited he had told her to "stop that nonsense."

Quietly she went upstairs. One of her little girls called: "Mummy, I heard what Daddy said; he talked so loudly. Does it mean that you have asked Jesus to come into your heart?"

"Yes, I have."

"Mummy, I should like to do it also."

Together they prayed; and she had the wonderful joy of bringing her little girl to the Lord Jesus on the very evening that she had made her decision for Him herself. Jesus was Victor once again!

The enemy, Satan, has much power to keep people under his sway; we must never underestimate it. But Jesus is stronger. Joined to Him we have a High Priest who is "touched with the feeling of our infirmities," who shares His resurrection power to overcome and who has at His command God's legions of angels.

TAPE RECORDING

Make the best possible use of your time. (Col. 4:5, Phillips)

Love is rich in finding opportunities. In Ashford, England, a young man asked me if I had anything against his recording my messages. Far from having objections to this, I am always thankful for every little microphone I see in the corner of the pulpit; for I know when God gives me a message it can help many more people than I am normally able to reach. The number is limited, after all, even though I travel all over the world. As every soul is precious in the loving eyes of Jesus, the more that are contacted with the Word of God the better. Tape recordings can be very useful in this.

On the last day in Ashford, I had four meetings and returned home feeling rather tired. I was not really fit enough to comply with this young man's request that I should fill the remaining side of his tape with one other message. However, we agreed that he should come early the next morning, when I would record another talk on to his tape and also learn some of his story.

He was full of zeal for souls but had no gift for speaking; thus, with his own money, he had bought a very good tape recorder and collected talks wherever he could find them. In his spare time he visited shut-ins with his tapes. He used them too in meetings in the surrounding small villages, in institutions and wherever he knew that people were happy to listen. He took a supply of my books with him to sell to those who like to read more of what the Lord has taught me in all my trips around the world and in the difficult class of life's school when I was a prisoner during the war.

Sometimes when I am the guest of someone who has a tape-recorder, I enjoy listening to messages of others very much; I have found that short tapes are often more useful than a whole hour-long sermon!

As Mr. Kenyon has so rightly challenged us, "Use your capital. You have in Jesus Christ boundless resources. We know what we are worth financially. In this grasping world of ours, we attempt to utilize all our possessions, but in the spiritual world how few of us know, possess and enjoy what our deed covers."

DEFEAT IN AN OLD LADIES' MEETING

Except a man be born again, he cannot see the kingdom of God.
(John 3:3)

In a dirty church room in England, we had a Bible class. (Why is it that so often old church buildings are so dirty? Do people forget that we are the heirs of the King of kings and representatives of His Majesty?) There were only twelve old ladies present, but this time I did not forget that every soul is precious in God's eyes. Although I was not originally asked to be the speaker, when a friend scheduled to give the message introduced me and asked me to give a talk, I agreed.

I began by explaining that being a Christian is not trying to live up to the Christian life but surrendering oneself to the pierced hand of Jesus. I demonstrated with a stick. Quite unable to stand upright on the floor by itself, when I held it steady with my hand, it did not fall, however light my touch. Jude says that the hand of Jesus will keep us from falling and, not only this, will present us blameless and with indescribable joy to the Father on that great day when Jesus reveals Himself (see Jude 24).

There are some who think that if a person is born into a

Christian family, he or she is automatically made a child of God. I told them that God has no grandchildren, but because He loves us so much, He wants to have our hearts. So each one born into a Christian family must make his own decision for Jesus Christ.

Others think that being a member of a church makes a person a Christian. Just as a piglet born in a palace is not a prince, so going to church does not make anyone a son of God. We have to be born into the family of God. To do this we must receive the Lord Jesus Christ. Then He gives us power to become the sons of God (see John 1:12).

Illustrating my talk with stories of my adventures on my world trips and experiences of prison life and underground work during the war, I told them that it is when we act on the Word of God that we find assurance of salvation. Those who believe on the name of the Son of God can know that they have everlasting life. Not by feeling but by acting on and believing in the Bible comes this blessed assurance that makes people say with Job, "I know that my Redeemer liveth."

As I continued I sensed that I was not making contact; these people were not tuned in on my wavelength. Only one lady smiled kindly each time I glanced her way. I prayed and prayed that the Lord would use me as a channel of His love and blessing, so my patience was kept at bay.

I felt unhappy and still could not rid myself of the horrible sensation that I was rubbing the fur of the cat in the wrong direction. I tried a joke but the only smiles displayed were on the two faces: the one who had invited me to speak and the one who smiled whenever I looked in her direction.

Afterward, as is the custom in every ladies' meeting in the British Isles, a cup of tea was served; so I endeavored to use this opportunity to come closer to my audience. Thanking the smiling lady I added, "You have encouraged me. I am sure you understood and accepted the message."

"That's kind of you to say so," was her surprising reply, "because I am deaf and did not hear or understand what you said. I smiled at you because of your sweet face."

What was I doing?

Another lady brought me a cup of tea, so I ventured, "Is it long since you made your decision for Christ?"

"I have been a member of this church for thirty-two years. Excuse me, I must go and serve the rest of the tea." Certainly she had not understood my talk.

A lady then came to sit on the chair beside me while she drank her tea. "I so enjoyed your talk," she said. At last, some encouragement! I tried to find out if she followed my line of thought.

"Did you receive Jesus a long time ago?" I queried.

"I never did, but I try hard to be a good Christian."

"Oh, you are like my illustration of the stick. Do you not agree that our sinful nature and the power of our enemy the devil are too strong for us? We can't stand alone by trying hard ourselves?"

"But there must be some trying on our part, I presume."

"The fruit of the Spirit is what we need." I opened my Phillips' translation at Galatians 5:22 and 23 and read, "The Spirit, however, produces in human life fruits such as these: love, joy, peace, patience, kindness, generosity, fidelity, tolerance, and self-control."

"You see," she exclaimed triumphantly, "now you have yourself said 'self-control.' We must control ourselves."

Meanwhile my companion was also trying to talk to some

of the women. She asked one, "Are you a child of God?"

"I hope so."

"On what do you base your hope?"

"On my good life; I am a decent woman. Nobody can tell me that I have ever done harm to anyone."

"Do you think your goodness is good enough for God? Jesus said that we should love our neighbors as ourselves and love God with all our hearts. Do you do that?"

"Oh, yes. I try. It is not as easy as your friend made out; we must be good theologians before we can understand it."

Yet another lady with whom she spoke remarked, "I have always been humble, not like that lady who spoke to us. She said she had a reservation in heaven—how dare she say such a thing! Spiritual pride, I call it!"

"But," my friend continued, "didn't Jesus say, 'I am the Way'? Doesn't God's Word say, 'These things have I written unto you that believe on the name of the Son of God; that ye may know that ye have eternal life' (1 John 5:13)?"

Was that whole afternoon a complete failure? I felt defeated. Before we left, one further little lady approached me.

"What must I do when I do not have enough faith?"

"Hudson Taylor, that great hero of faith, has said that it is not a great faith that we need, just faith in a great God. Have you a few minutes to spare?" She had; so I opened my Bible to Isaiah 5:6 and read, "All we like sheep have gone astray." Then I said, "Have you?"

"Yes, I went my own way."

"And the Lord hath laid on him [Jesus] the iniquity of us all," I read on. "Jesus finished all that had to be done; now all we have to do is receive His salvation. Did you understand that while I was speaking? Those words from John 1:12?"

"Yes, I think I understood."

"Will you say 'Yes' to Jesus? And if you mean it will you shake hands with me?"

She gave me her hand. I trust that she was the one for whom I had had to go to the old ladies' meeting in that dirty church room. Their self-improvement and efforts were so much to them, self-reformation, self-righteousness. But God demands, and gives, regeneration, His righteousness, His life.

GUIDED AVAILABILITY

He that cometh to me shall never hunger. (John 6:35)

Germany after the war: packed trains with people climbing through the windows to get a ride in the overcrowded coaches!

From a short distance I watched the fighting, struggling mass, but had no longing at all to press myself into the overflowing carriages. The train drew out of the station leaving behind at least one-third of the passengers. I had to be in Kassel that evening and was left wondering what to do.

I noticed an American train on the other side of the track bound for that very town. I made my way to it and found an empty compartment—what quietness and rest. Not being an American I did not know whether I even had the right to travel on this train, but I hoped for the best.

A sergeant entered at one of the stations where the train stopped, so I asked him if it were in order for me, a Dutch woman, to travel on that particular train. He assured me it was quite right, and thus I was given a good opportunity to speak to him. I prayed for guidance and wisdom.

It was not difficult to come to the most important subject, for the young man quickly told me that he had a longing for peace with God. "My buddy tells me that I must be
converted, but I don't understand that word. I know what
converted bombers are," he added jokingly, "we have plenty
of them in America!"

"Do these bombers have the same engines as before?" I
asked, revealing my ignorance but hoping for a good illustration. It came, but not the way I thought.

"Yes, everything is the same: instead of guns and bombs
though there are seats for passengers. Of course the crew is
different: the civil airline pilots take the place of the airforce
ones."

"When you ask Jesus Christ to take over your life, He
gives you a new heart. Instead of anxiety He gives peace;
instead of sins He gives the Holy Spirit and the fruit of the
Spirit. Instead of self, Jesus becomes the Pilot—a very able
Pilot indeed."

"What must I do to be converted?"

"Conversion is to turn about: 180 degrees. The original
attitude of man is that he lives away from God. After conversion you live with your face toward God."

"Is it as easy as that? Mustn't I first try to be a better guy
than I am?"

"No! When you turn to Jesus, He does the job. After
you have turned 180 degrees, you are not going on in your
own strength any longer; you have with you the greatest
Friend the world has ever seen. You do not give yourself
salvation; it is a gift from Jesus. He is the Way, the Truth
and the Life."

I read to him from Philippians 3:14 in the Phillips' translation: "'I leave the past behind and with hands outstretched to whatever lies ahead I go straight for the goal—my reward the honor of my high calling by God in Christ Jesus.' It is a great new beginning. The Bible shows you that Jesus is the Way and that He died for us all, doing everything that was necessary for our salvation.

"But salvation is a gift: and you must take it. Believe in the Lord Jesus Christ and you will be saved. Surrender all to your new Pilot; then confess your sins—all your guns and bombs must be removed from the plane. When we repent and confess our sins, God is faithful and just to forgive and the blood of Jesus cleanses our hearts.

"Now the Bible is your Book. Study it and you will see how rich you are. I have heard it said that there are five thousand promises in the Bible; in Jesus all are 'yea and amen.' It is your checkbook with all the checks made out in your name and signed by Jesus."

The sergeant bowed his head and prayed, "Jesus, I turn 180 degrees. I receive You as my Pilot; come into my bomber and take away my sins. You know, Lord, what there is in my heart. Make it clean."

I knew why I had to travel in that American train.

CRIPPLED LEGS

When he ascended upon high, he . . . gave gifts unto men.
(Eph. 4:8)

When one does a lot of traveling, there is no time for sickness or accidents. Yet my prison experiences had affected my body, and I also have been "a long time young." But the Lord restores my health and strength, and daily I enjoy His constant care. He knows that it is difficult to work when one feels unwell.

Giving too much attention to little symptoms also plays into the hands of the enemy, who uses it to depress us until we see things out of all proportion to their true value. I will not say that every illness is out of the plan of God. After all, we are training for higher service; and I know that suffering can be part of that training.

Some years ago my sister, Nollie, died. We had been related not only by ties of blood but by an unusually deep spiritual understanding with each other. It had been a very real sacrifice to leave her when I began my journeyings all over the world. I always counted the days and weeks until we should meet again. Although her health was bad, yet she never asked me to stay with her or to shorten my absences from our home. She was never a burden to me.

Her letters were a constant inspiration to me; and after her death I received three—one written the day she had died. I thought that I had quite accepted her going Home, but deep in my heart there was a mourning which affected me more than I realized. Thus, feeling tired and depressed, conscious that I needed a rest, I went to Holland to spend five days at Zonneduin, what was then my international guest house in Bloemendaal.

Plane travel was postponed because of stormy weather so I went by train. Arriving in Haarlem I had a bad fall in the station and felt intense pain in my hip. I prayed, "Lord Jesus, lay Your healing hand on my hip." Immediately the pain was eased a little, but I could not move. The police helped to carry me to a car. In hospital the doctor diagnosed a broken hip and feared it would be many months before I should be able to walk again. However an X-ray revealed that nothing was broken, and I was allowed to continue to Zonneduin to be nursed by my friends.

So I had to lie quietly in my bed! I was dependent on the help of others for everything. The sudden change from an active life to one of complete inactivity was too much for me. There was rebellion in my heart. It is a good thing to stay put when one is ill, but I was not ill at all—merely reduced to absolute immobility by that stupid wounded hip! I fear my friends suffered because of my bad humor and demanding attitude.

"Is there not someone who has the special gift of healing?" I asked. They indeed knew someone and sent for this brother to come and lay hands on me (see Mark 16:18 and James 5:14–15). He asked me if there was any unconfessed sin. I did not have to dig deep to find my demanding attitude towards my nurse. Then a miracle happened.

No, my hip was not healed. But during the prayer and laying on of hands by the brother, a joy unspeakable entered my heart; I experienced the peace beyond all understanding such as I had never known before. I felt as if the ocean of God's love surrounded me. In that moment the sense of mourning for Nollie disappeared and it has never come back.

The Lord knew I was going to face new fights with dark powers in the coming months, and this was a reinforcement by the Holy Spirit. The Lord gave me power which I should certainly have missed if I had continued with my unrepenting darkness which had enveloped my heart.

"Can I walk now?" I asked this servant of the Lord.

"You are desiring but a cupful; you were given an ocean," was his reply.

In fact I could not yet walk; but the joy of the Lord was in my heart. Some people call this "The Baptism," others "The Second Blessing." I don't mind what they call it, for I believe not only in a second blessing but third and more blessings. Our hearts are so small! Several times I had to say to the Lord, "Not any more, Lord; my heart will burst for joy."

Ten days later I was able to leave for Germany, walking with the aid of a stick. I thanked the Lord that I had always been able to walk normally, for this experience taught me how much we take for granted and how little we appreciate what we have until we lose it. Being in prison, for example, gave me an appreciation and enjoyment of doors which I can open from both sides!

When I arrived in Bodenhagen, a small town in Hanover, it had been snowing and freezing; the ground was like a skating rink. I was the only passenger to alight. Between me and the station another train was standing so that when my train drew out nobody could see me. Unable to walk on the slippery ground, I waited until the other train departed. I then saw to my astonishment that everyone had gone. Although I called, no one answered.

There I stood. What was I to do? Not knowing that my friends, on their way to meet me, were delayed by icy roads, I could but pray and surrender myself afresh to the Lord. I was not afraid, for there was peace in my heart; but how glad I was when my friends arrived and drove me home. For several weeks I was still dependent on the help of my stick.

Later, while I was using my extra leg, I arrived in a small village where the church was built on a hill. The church bells were already ringing, and the people decided not to stop them until I reached the church. I could not hurry, for the way was uphill on a rocky, mountain road. I leaned on the arm of my companion, but we went very slowly. I knew I had to reach the top, but it seemed as if we were held back— almost like a nightmare!

The landscape was a lovely Christmas picture; The windows of the church were lit while the moonlight glistened on the snow, giving a sparkling clear visibility. The congregation within the church started to sing. Their voices, accompanied by the ringing church bells, were lovely as they floated across the valley. Suddenly a group of young girls ran toward us from the church, jumping and springing carefree over the snow. "We have come to help you!" they shouted. The air was filled with laughter. Some pushed, some pulled, and my progress up the hill was much quicker.

When I reached the church, I saw that, as in so many of the old churches in Germany, there was a very high pulpit. I asked for permission to stand at the foot of it, for my tired legs did not feel equal to the strain of going up the steps of this very, very high pulpit. Tiredness enlarges problems out of all proportion.

But now the bells were silent. Quietly the Lord worked that evening. He gave me a message challenging people to come to Jesus Christ. "Jesus is longing to bless, but we must stretch out our hands to take. Come and repent; Jesus will forgive and cleanse us from our sins." This was my burden.

Afterward, tired but happy, I descended the same hill. This was almost harder than climbing up, but many of my young girls helped me faithfully, placing themselves in front of me to keep me from sliding. We had lots of fun, those young rascals and I!

After a while the strain began to tell on me, so I decided to take a short rest. I shall never forget that moment. We were silent with the quietness of the snowy mountainous landscape around us. We could feel the presence of God. Softly I asked a girl, "What did the Lord say to you this evening?"

"He told me that I was not a good Christian."

"Will you surrender your whole life to the Lord? He has bought you with so high a price—His precious blood. Give Him His money's worth. Don't try to be better, but lay your hands in the loving hands of Jesus; He will be your Guide."

Then I turned to another, "Have you ever received the Lord Jesus as your Savior?"

"No, I haven't, but I will now."

"Bring all your sins to Him and trust Him as your Savior and Victor."

"And what about you?" I said to a third.

"I have always been a faithful member of the Sunday school and gone to church; but now I see that I must make a decision for Jesus Christ. I too will do it now." It was not difficult for her to speak to the Lord Jesus, for it was not imagination that made us feel the angels surrounding us. We were very close to heaven.

All the girls surrendered their hearts and lives to the Lord Jesus, while I could only thank God for my crippled legs which had given this blessed "after-meeting" in the snow.

Ten

The Palace of Plenty

I am come that they might have life,
and that they might have it more abundantly. (John 10:10)

When the Bible authors try to describe the riches we have in Jesus, it is as if they cannot find sufficient human words to express the glimpses of the glory which they have been given and of the joy which they have known. They write of "Love which passeth knowledge" (Eph. 3:19); "Joy unspeakable" (1 Pet. 1:8); "Peace which passeth understanding" (Phil. 4:7); "Unsearchable riches" (Eph. 3:8); "Innumerable company of angels" (Heb. 12:22); "Unspeakable gift" (2 Cor. 9:15); "Plenteous in mercy" (Ps. 10:8); "Good measure, pressed down, and shaken together, and running over" (Luke 6:38).

Do not be afraid to aim too high for as C.S. Lewis said, "We are often like children satisfied with a puddle in the backyard, when they have been invited for a day at the ocean."

The story goes that in a Scottish bank there were forty million pounds in unclaimed deposits! How many unclaimed deposits there are in the Bible! Are we professors or possessors? Remember that every promise of God is backed by the golden reserves of the bank of heaven, available to us here and now, in good times or bad. When the worst happens, yet the best remains.

Another has described the Christian life as a walk into a splendid palace through marvellous antechambers. We cannot go into the second room if we have not passed through the first; we cannot reach the fifth if we are not willing to enter the fourth.

Let me share with you the palace rooms which I have found on life's journey towards that final, exceeding magnificent room, the throne room of heaven. We cannot be present in all the rooms at the same time. If we are in the kitchen or the bedroom, we are not in the living room; but we know that the doors to these other rooms are open. If sometimes we find a door closed to us, then we have only to knock and it will be opened. Jesus is the Door and He is on street level. When we put our hands into His, He leads us from one room to the next.

> I count everything as loss compared to the priceless privilege—the overwhelming preciousness, the surpassing worth and supreme advantage—of knowing Christ Jesus my Lord, and of progressively becoming more deeply and intimately acquainted with Him. (Phil. 3:8, Amp.)

The First Room: Rebirth

Except a man be born again, he cannot see the kingdom of God.
(John 3:3)

Throughout this book I have mentioned how this room is entered. We may become members of the family of God only by being born into His kingdom. It is a mystery, but when we act on the words of the Bible, we discover that the promises which God has given to us in His Book have not been made in vain but are truly meant by Him.

What must we do? In John 1:12 we read that in receiving Jesus Christ He gives us power to become children of God. Some people think this is not only the beginning but the end. They say with joy, "By grace I am made a child of God. Now the purpose of my life is fulfilled and there is nothing more for me to do."

True, it means coming from darkness into light, but it is far from being the end. Rather it is the great beginning. When we enter the kingdom, the Lord throws wide open the doors of the treasure house and bids us come to His storehouse and take with boldness. We do not even have to start at the bottom but at the top, the cross where Jesus finished His blessed work. All promises are fulfilled in Christ, "yea and amen."

The many who think of conversion as the final target remind me of the boy who fell out of his bed. When his mother asked him how it happened, he replied, "Mummy, I think I fell asleep too close to the place where I got into bed." When, after conversion, we "fall asleep" we become backsliders. To avoid this from happening we must read the Bible. We must have fellowship with the Lord, pray, testify and act on the Word of God in order to learn of its great riches in plenty. Thus come quickly into the second room. We must not linger in the first chamber but press on and go forward.

The Second Room: Assurance of Salvation

You that believe on the name of the Son of God
may know that ye have eternal life. (1 John 5:13)

My father was eighty-four years old when he was taken into the prison at Scheveningen during the Second World War. He was arrested because he had saved the lives of many Jewish people. When others warned him of the dangers of this rescue work he always answered, "I know that if I am put into prison I shall be too old to stand the life there. Even so, I shall think of it as an honor to give my life for God's ancient people, the Jews."

As he entered the prison he said, "Corrie, the best is yet to be." In ten days he was dead. Prison walls separated him from all his children—three daughters, one son and one grandson—all in the same building. It had been many years before, when he was only seventeen, that he had entered the second room of God's palace; so when he was eighty-four he could say so confidently to me, "The best is yet to be."

What peace there is in this room!

In the concentration camp we were sometimes permitted the luxury of a hot shower. More than a hundred prisoners at a time would be taken into a room where suddenly many showers would stream from the ceiling. It was such a blessed relief to feel the hot water on our bodies after the cramping in our barracks, built for four hundred but housing fourteen hundred prisoners. The rumor went around that this shower room was also a gas chamber. This proved untrue; nevertheless we believed it. Before the water started to run, the tension was terrible. Would it be water today . . . or gas?

At such moments one looks death in the eyes. But Jesus had given me such assurance of salvation in the second room that I could look up to Him and say, "'O death, where is thy sting? O grave, where is thy victory?'" I thanked God for the victory of my Lord Jesus Christ which was just as much mine.

THE THIRD ROOM: THE SURRENDERED WILL

I delight to do thy will, O my God. (Ps. 40:8)

I used to be afraid of this room. I was like the boy in the story of the famous tightrope walker, Blondin, who, when asked if he believed that Blondin could wheel him safely over Niagara Falls in his wheelbarrow, replied, "I certainly do, for I have seen you with my own eyes; and I have never seen anything so splendid before."

"When I make another trip over the rope, will you get into the wheelbarrow and come with me?"

"No, I wouldn't dream of it!"

That boy believed in the ability of the tightrope walker but would not trust himself to him. (For that matter, neither would I!)

The enemy tells us that surrendering our will to God is taking the same sort of risk involved by traveling over that rope in the wheelbarrow. But he is a liar. It means to be safe in the arms of Jesus. I did not trust myself to make that decision. It appeared to me that I would have to say, "I will surrender my will. I will be faithful to my surrender. I will always. . . ." This was far too much "I."

When in New Zealand I met Chris Lethbridge, from whom I learned what a surrendered will meant. Chris was a theological student who had fractured his neck in a swimming accident which had left him paralyzed from his neck down. But his brain was unimpaired and he was very intelligent.

I had the joy of spending a Christmas vacation in the same home where he kindly helped me correct my last book, *Not Good If Detached.* He turned the pages with a small stick which he held between his teeth, the stick having a little rubber hand at the end. He was a true Christian, but at this time came a testing of his faith. He began to doubt God's vision and love. Did God care?

"Why doesn't the Lord heal me?" he asked, unable to surrender his sufferings. But there came a monent one day when I heard him pray, "O God, make me willing to be willing."

That was surrender! Now even the surrender was in God's hands. What a glad and beaming face Chris had after that hour. How the Lord could use him as a channel of light in the hospital where he had to be. And now? He is a minister, mightily used of God.

Is the cross heavy? Surrender. "The best is yet to be."

THE FOURTH ROOM: TOTAL SURRENDER

The price was in fact the life-blood of Christ.
(1 Pet. 1:19, Phillips)

When I was arrested by the Gestapo, I was obliged to surrender to a cruel enemy. I was not allowed to take the slightest initiative about anything but had to obey the people in whose hands my life was. How I rebelled in my heart against that! But there was no choice! I had to obey and lead a life surrendered totally to the enemy.

I once read about an event which occurred at the end of the American Civil War. President Lincoln was standing with several generals before a table on which was spread a map of the States. One general after another made proposals. "We will surrender this part of our State to your government, but this little part we will keep for ourselves." After each of them had made similar offers, the President put his hand on the map simply saying, "Gentlemen, my government will have all."

So often we are like those generals: We are willing to surrender our whole lives, families and money to the Lord, yet we have one little "but"—a little corner to keep all to ourselves. Jesus says, "My Father will have all."

Then is God a dictator? No, He is a loving Father, but does He not have a legal right to own us 100%? We are bought with a very high price—the precious blood of His only Son, Jesus.

Before the Second World War, I had a watch and jewelry shop. Suppose I had sold you a watch with a gold bracelet but while I was wrapping your watch, I had removed the bracelet so that you would have found only the watch when you arrived home. What do you think would have happened? Why, you would have warned all your friends not to buy from Corrie ten Boom. "She isn't honest," you would have said. "She doesn't give you your money's worth."

Have you given God His money's worth? He paid a high price for you.

Sometimes in the concentration camp at Ravensbruck, we had to stand stripped of all our clothes. The first time this happened I said to my sister, Betsie, "This is worse than anything else we have suffered." Never had we felt so cold, humiliated and ashamed, so utterly miserable.

Then suddenly, as though I saw Jesus on the cross, I realized for the first time that He had hung there naked. The Bible says, "They took his garments." Now, with my own suffering, I was able to understand a fraction of the passion, of the shame, that Jesus had borne for me, for everyone.

I put my arm around Betsie and said, "Jesus hung on the cross naked. They took away His garments when He hung there for you and me, bearing our punishment." This gave us strength to bear our own small sufferings as we were thankful to Him for His.

> *Did e'er such love and sorrow meet,*
> *Or thorns compose so rich a crown? . . .*
> *Love so amazing, so divine,*
> *Demands my soul, my life, my all.*
>
> Isaac Watts

Piet de Koning was one of the young boys arrested and tortured by the Gestapo in Holland. When his sister visited him during Lent, he remarked to her, "This is the most blessed Passion-time of all my life. Never have I been so thankful for or realized so much Jesus' sufferings for my sins."

Do we live in the fourth room? As a test for the surrendered life, here is a question we can ask ourselves: "Can I pray for everything?"

During the twenty-five years I owned a jeweler's shop, I made many friends in Switzerland from whom I bought watches. On one occasion I had bought three watches and slipped them into a corner of my suitcase to avoid the high duty on such goods that the Dutch customs would demand on my return. My experiences in the underground movement had taught me well how to hide things!

Before boarding the plane on my return trip I prayed, "Lord, will you give us a good trip and a safe journey: good flying weather, skill and ability to the pilot, a safe landing. And, Lord, help me to smug. . . ."

I could not finish my prayer for smuggling safety. For, in the moment of prayer, I realized that I could not pray for a sin. Smuggling is stealing. I had been very stupid and wrong not to see this before. My awareness of the impossibility of praying for it showed me that it was a sin.

Is there anything for which you cannot pray? Can you pray for that book you are reading, for that club membership, for the way you earn your living? Can you honestly pray for God's blessing on the way you use your spare time? Or your sex life; or your friendships? Is there anything for which you cannot or will not pray? Then there is sin. Your heart is not in tune with God if there is a sin in your life that you refuse to give up. But He assured us that His yoke is easy, His burden light.

THE FIFTH ROOM: THE FULLNESS OF THE HOLY SPIRIT

Be filled with the Spirit. (Eph. 5:18)

We can never enter here if we have not passed through the room of total surrender. Some people imagine this is a room for the spiritual aristocracy, yet it is indeed the birthright of every believer. The moment we enter the first room we receive the Holy Spirit, and He witnesses "with our spirit, that we are children of God" (Rom. 8:16).

But Paul tells Christians, "Be filled with the Spirit." There is all the difference between possessing a house and living in it. So many Christians live on the wrong side of Pentecost.

When I was released from my imprisonment in a concentration camp, I could say to my friends in Holland, "There are three great realities in my life." They thought I would say, "One is the cruelty of mankind." Although my body bore the marks of this reality, nevertheless by the grace of God I saw things from His point of view. "God's love is the greatest reality; second, God's promises and third, His commandments." God has no suggestions, only commandments—with the sweetest command in Ephesians 5:18: "Be filled with the Spirit."

Why is this so important? God the Father glorifies Jesus in heaven, but the Holy Spirit glorifies Jesus on earth. He has no other dwelling place than in our hearts. When we are filled with the Holy Spirit, we then are used to glorify Jesus.

However, the Holy Spirit cannot and will not live in a dirty house. When there are unconfessed sins in our hearts, He cannot dwell there. What can we do with such sins as pride, self-pity, jealousy, sexual impurity, criticism, inferiority feelings, dishonesty, unpaid debts, etc.? God's faithfulness and truth are the guarantees of our forgiveness when the blood of Jesus Christ cleanses us from all the sins we confess. 1 John 1:7–9 is the first aid for the sinning Christian, but His blood will never cleanse an excuse.

After we have brought our last sin to the Lord, we must surrender. Then we can claim the fullness of the Holy Spirit. Claiming is an act of faith based on the express promise in God's Word. As we believe, so we receive.

The Holy Spirit must have preeminence. He handles all our affairs. The early teachers did not wait for a period of years until the young converts had been thoroughly disheartened and demoralized by disappointment and failure. They taught straightaway the overcoming, victorious life through the fullness of the Holy Spirit.

Before them John the Baptist had pointed out two things

when he saw Christ: First, "Behold the Lamb of God, which taketh away the sin of the world." Second, "The same is he which baptizeth with the Holy Ghost."

It was Jesus Himself who said that the greatest proof of His own love to the world would be demonstrated through His promised power of the Holy Spirit.

THE SIXTH ROOM: ABIDING IN CHRIST

Abide in him; that, when he shall appear, we may have confidence, and not be ashamed before him at his coming.
(1 John 2:28)

This is the room of John 15: the vine and the branches—the room of fruit, more fruit, much fruit. Here is the joy of the Lord: "My joy may be in you that your joy may be full" (see v.11). When we are attached to Jesus, His love is our love and His joy our joy.

In Korea, from a shed made of old cardboard and rags, I heard a woman singing this amazing chorus: "Where Jesus is, 'tis heaven there." Here is a room which contains plentiful supplies of love for one's enemies.

A penny cannot float on water by itself; the law of gravity will cause it to sink. If the penny is attached to a piece of pine wood it will float. The law of gravity has not ceased, but the law which makes the wood float is stronger. By the same token, when I try to be good and to love my enemies, I discover my sinful nature and the power of the devil make me sin. When I am connected to Jesus His love and goodness become mine.

At the close of a meeting in Berlin some time ago, a man came into the inquiry room. He appeared depressed and downhearted and had great difficulty in saying what it was that troubled him so deeply. I became impatient with him, asking rather abruptly, "Come along, what's your problem? I don't have much time. Let's talk together; perhaps I can help you?" His answer made me tremble.

"I was one of the guards at Ravensbruck," he replied, "during the time you were a prisoner there. A few months ago I was saved and brought all my sins to Jesus. He has forgiven me, and I have prayed that I might be allowed to ask forgiveness from one of my victims. I know everything about the transportation of the Dutch women—you numbered about a thousand—from Vught in Holland in 1944. Can you forgive me for my cruelties?"

At that moment it was as though a wave of God's love streamed through my heart; and I said to him, "Brother, I forgive you with my whole heart!" I took his hand—the hand that had been so cruel.

Could I have done that with my love? No! But with the love of Jesus in my heart, I was able to do so. Without Him I would have hated this man, but connected to Jesus I could joyfully love him with God's plentiful love.

It was Jesus who prayed on the cross, "Father, forgive them; for they know not what they do" (Luke 23:4).

> *So nigh, so very nigh to God,*
> *I cannot nearer be,*
> *For in the person of His Son*
> *I am as near as He.*
>
> *So dear, so very dear to God,*
> *More dear I cannot be,*
> *The love wherewith He loves the Son,*
> *Such is His love for me.*

The Seventh Room: Victory Over Sin

Thanks be to God, which giveth us the victory through our Lord Jesus Christ. (1 Cor. 15:57)

The victorious life is the normal one for a Christian. Sin finds power through unbelief which uses the excuse, "I'm only human." It is the same attitude of mind as that adopted by the pickpocket who said, "I'm a good Christian. Once upon a time I would have stolen fifty watches every month. Since I have been converted, I steal only four or five."

In the seventh room we see that every temptation offers an occasion for victory. It is a signal to fly the flag of our Victor, an opportunity to make the tempter know anew that he is defeated. The prince of this world is judged.

In this room the joy of our salvation is also restored (Ps. 51:12). No condemnation can hang over the head of those who are in Christ Jesus, for the new spiritual principle of life "in" Christ lifts me out of the old vicious circle of sin and death (see Rom. 8:1).

Although we know about this vicious circle of sin and try again and again to live up to the Christian life (indeed we may be successful for a time) yet we fall because of our sinful nature; and the power of the enemy keeps us on the deadly treadmill of sin. Jesus came to lift us out of it and to put us into the blessed circle of the Holy Spirit.

If we then sin we confess it immediately; and "We find God utterly straightforward—he forgives our sins" (Phillips) and the blood which His Son shed for us keeps us clean from all sin. Should we fail again, our Advocate lives and His blood is available to cleanse us from our sins.

After confession and cleansing we can then be filled with the Holy Spirit, for there is room for Him to dwell in us. We must get ourselves into the good habit of instantly confessing our sins and not wait until it is time to be in church or when we have our evening prayers.

When I was speaking in a church in Japan, I asked the pastor to make the preliminaries short. (Later I understood that it is not permissible to refer to the equally important part of the service—hymns, prayers and offertory—as "preliminaries.") The pastor agreed. Nevertheless he took his time.

The service began at 10:30, and at 11:30 we had a long prayer preceding the offering, with yet another prayer after it. I looked at my watch, feeling very impatient. But impatience is sin; so at 11:30 I confessed my sin and asked forgiveness.

At 11:30 I experienced that my Advocate lives at the right hand of the Father. I could imagine Jesus saying to the Father, "I take upon Myself this impatience of Corrie's." Thus at 11:30 the blood of Jesus cleansed me from all my impatience so that I honestly could think and pray, "Why, this must be a blessed collection; it's been prayed for twice."

Why have I stressed 11:30? As I have an Advocate, so I have an accuser. Perhaps Satan accused me to the Father at 11:35; but I had nothing to fear for God would have said, "I know all about it. Corrie ten Boom was here five minutes ago." I often think it happens like this. Let the devil accuse, but it is too late, for God Himself has cast all my sins into the very deeps of the sea, forgiven and forgotten (see Mic. 7:19).

Another point to remember: Satan accuses us to our own hearts as well as before God. How many Christians listen to him, pray and even sing themselves into feelings of guilt and self-accusation. Instant confession means instant forgiveness and cleansing, rendering the accuser impotent.

Does this sound too easy? Is not the fight one of strife and wrestling? Does not Scripture say "Ye have not yet resisted unto blood, striving against sin" (Heb. 12:4)? Yes, it is a tremendous struggle in which we need the whole armor of God until the very last minute of our lives, but it is always available in the person of Jesus Christ.

Some Christians laugh about their sins instead of weeping. But we are told: "Be ye perfect" (Matt. 5:48)—holiness is not an idea or suggestion, it is a definite command. There is no license for man's sinning or amusement in it. "I beseech you therefore, brethren, by the mercies of God, that ye present your bodies a living sacrifice, holy, acceptable unto God, which is your reasonable service" (Rom. 12:1). Bring your sins to the source of forgiveness and cleansing. Don't play with them.

Then look forward with Paul: "I leave the past behind and with hands outstretched to whatever lies ahead I go straight for the goal—my reward the honor of my high calling by God in Christ Jesus" (Phil. 3:14, Phillips).

> It is a battle of faith. Jesus is always victorious. In heaven they are praising Him all the time for His victory. Whatever may be our experience of failure, He is never defeated. His power is boundless. We have only to get into a right relationship with Him and we shall see His power being demonstrated in our hearts and lives and service, and His victorious life will fill us and overflow through us to others. That is revival in its essence. (Roy Hession, *The Calvary Road*)

THE EIGHTH ROOM: HEART REST

We are asking God that you may see things, as it were from his point of view by being given spiritual insight and understanding.
(Col. 1:9, Phillips)

This is the room where you see things from God's viewpoint!

When my sister Nollie, the mother of six children, was arrested by the Nazis after they had found two Jews in her house, I tried to contact her. She was the first of our family to be taken, and our concern was very great.

Seeing her come out of the door toward a prison van, I broke through the barrier of policemen, ran to her and flung my arms around her. Smiling into my sad face she only said, "God is love."

Had she said, "Can you understand that a God of love would allow the enemy to bring me here when I was helping His people?" my human reason and emotion would have responded thus. But the reality of God's love was as real to her in prison, remaining unquestioned.

That prison van was dark, but suddenly there appeared a beam of light. Nollie had a little pencil concealed in her hair (All of us tried to hide one somewhere on our persons, for a pencil is treasure to a prisoner; and we never knew when or if we would be arrested). With it she wrote on the wall, "Jesus is Victor."

Five other women joined her in the cell and regarded her happy face with amazement. "Don't you cry?" they asked, confessing how they had wept much when they first entered prison.

Nollie answered, "No, I am not crying, for I know that

God does not make mistakes, even allowing the Nazis to bring me here."

Nollie was in this eighth room during all that time: peace of heart, rest of mind. It was His calm that was her strength and that helped her face her calamities.

As the songwriter said, "Where Jesus is: 'tis heaven there." Rest in the Lord is independent of our external circumstances; it is a trusting, triumphant relationship with the Lord Himself.

What a palace! What plenty! "O taste and see that the Lord is good: blessed is the man that trusteth in him" (Ps. 34:8).

Eleven

A Tramp for the Lord

Work, for the night cometh.

How the enemy tries to make everything work out for the worst! During the time of which I am thinking, I was feeling discouraged—not a little bit, but very much so. A series of little incidents led to frustration.

In my journeyings I often have to cross borders between countries, and knowing that smuggling is sin, I do not do it. The first irritation came through an encounter with a customs' official when he asked me if I had anything to declare. I replied, "Yes, nylon stockings," and put them on top of my luggage to show him.

"There are four pairs here," he said. "You told me one pair!"

"No, I did not."

He took my suitcases and gave them such a thorough inspection that it took at least an hour. He tried all the little boxes for false bottoms, so minute was his examination. I felt offended and unhappy. He found nothing for all his search, so I paid the duty on the four pairs of stockings. But the depression and unhappiness remained.

Later I understood why this incident had made me feel so upset: I had not surrendered my self-righteousness. I was so sure of my own honesty that I suffered from the consequence of wounded pride. It is easier to surrender one's sins rather than one's virtues!

Unaware of the reason for my depression, I then discovered that I had missed my plane connection due to the delay in the customs' office and was forced to sleep on a couch in the women's room at the airport. However, I am a good sleeper, so I enjoyed a sound slumber.

When I awoke, the amazed cleaner, sweeping the floor around my couch, said with admiration, "How wonderful to be able to sleep so soundly with such noise going on around you!"

Eventually the plane on which I traveled flew into a storm making me feel airsick. Then the night following my arrival there was an earthquake. I hate earthquakes. I was reminded of wartime when the bombs fell all around. Every minute I used to have the dreadful feeling that each moment would be my last. It was not panic but the uncertainty, the insecurity.

When I remember these circumstances which contributed to my feeling of discouragement I am now ashamed; but this was not the end.

The kind people who should have arranged my meetings greeted my arrival with: "We thought you needed a holiday and a rest, so we have not organized anything." Sometimes I am given this sort of encouragement, but it is often an excuse for their inactivity, which I do not appreciate.

The room which my hosts gave me was small and without a table for writing. This final small inconvenience should not have disturbed me; I was used to writing on my knee.

The reason was not hard to find as self-pity came into my heart. It is a nasty little demon who always starts his talks with "Poor Corrie."

This time it began: "Why must you always live out of your suitcases? Stay at home, and then you won't have trouble with customs' officials, passports, luggage, plane connections and other things. Every night you will be able to sleep in the same comfortable bed; and there are no earthquakes in Holland. After all, you are no longer young; you've lived like a tramp for fifteen years. Nobody is indispensable; let someone else do the work. There's plenty for you to do in Holland."

That day I saw he was absolutely right. Having listened to his advice, I wrote to Bloemendaal, where my friend was manageress of an international guest house and where, at that time, I had a room kept for me with all my own furniture:

> I believe the time has now come for me to work in Holland. I am tired of all this traveling, and I cannot stand having wheels beneath me any longer. Will you arrange to have a desk—a big one—put in front of the window in my room, and an easy chair—a very easy one—on the right. . . .

In my fantasy I had worked out a lovely dream, and thus I wrote. After I had posted this letter, I made plans to cancel my appointments. Everyone would know that I needed to go home. Had not many said, "My, you must be tired!"

Everything would have gone all right—or perhaps it would be truthful to say *all wrong*—had I not read from one of Amy Carmichael's books, *Things as They Are*,* that evening. Do you know her story, or rather dream, which the Lord

---

* Now out of print. Permission to quote given by the Dohnavur Fellowship.

gave her in India?

It all began because she had read:

> If you could only know what one feels on finding one-self . . . where the least ray of the Gospel has not penetrated! If those friends who blame . . . could see from afar what we see, and feel what we feel, they would be the first to wonder that those redeemed by Christ should be so backward in devotion and know so little of the spirit of self-sacrifice. They would be ashamed of the hesitations that hinder us. . . . We must remember that it was not by interceding for the world in glory that Jesus saved it. He gave Himself. Our prayers for the evangelization of the world are but a bitter irony so long as we only give of the superfluity, and draw back before the sacrifice of ourselves. (M. Francois Coillard, Africa)

> Someone must go; and if no one else will go, he who hears the call must go; I hear the call, for indeed God has brought it before me on every side, and go I must. (Rev. Henry Watson Fox, India)

From reading and thinking on these lines, Amy Carmichael goes on to write:

> The tom-toms thumped straight on all night, and the darkness shuddered round me like a living, feeling thing. I could not go to sleep, so I lay awake and looked; and I saw, as it seemed, this:
>
> That I stood on a grassy sward, and at my feet a preci-pice broke sheer down into infinite space. I looked, but saw no bottom; only cloud shapes, black and furiously coiled, and great shadow-shrouded hollows, and unfathomable depths. Back I drew, dizzy at the depth.
>
> Then I saw forms of people moving single file along the grass. They were making for the edge. There was a woman with a baby in her arms and another little child holding on

to her dress. She was on the very verge. Then I saw that she was blind. She lifted her foot for the next step . . . it trod air. She was over, and the children with her. Oh, the cry as they went over!

Then I saw more streams of people flowing from all quarters. All were blind, stone blind; all made straight for the precipice edge. There were shrieks as they suddenly knew themselves falling, and a tossing up of helpless arms, catching, clutching at empty air. But some went over quietly, and fell without a sound.

Then I wondered, with a wonder that was simply agony, why no one stopped them at the edge. I could not. I was glued to the ground, and I could not call; though I strained and tried, only a whisper could come.

Then I saw that along the edge there were sentries set at intervals. But the intervals were far too great; there were wide, unguarded gaps between. And over these gaps the people fell in their blindness, quite unwarned; and the green grass seemed blood-red to me, and the gulf yawned like the mouth of hell.

Then I saw, like a little picture of peace, a group of people under some trees, with their backs turned towards the gulf. They were making daisy chains. Sometimes when a piercing shriek cut the quiet air and reached them it disturbed them, and they thought it rather a vulgar noise. And if one of their number started up and wanted to go and do something to help, then all the others would pull that one down. "Why should you get so excited about it? You must wait for a definite call to go! You have not finished your daisy chains yet. It would be really selfish," they said, "to leave us to finish the work alone."

There was another group. It was made up of people whose great desire was to get more sentries out; but they found that very few wanted to go, and sometimes there were no sentries set for miles and miles of the edge.

Once a girl stood alone in her place, waving the people back; but her mother and other relations called, and reminded her that her furlough was due; she must not break the rules. And being tired and needing a change she had to go and rest for a while; but no one was sent to guard her gap, and over and over the people fell, like a waterfall of souls.

Once a child caught a tuft of grass that grew at the very brink of the gulf; it clung convulsively, and it called—but nobody seemed to hear. Then the roots of the grass gave way, and with a cry the child went over, its two little hands still holding tight to the torn-off bunch of grass. And the girl who longed to be back in her gap thought she heard the little one cry, and she sprang up and wanted to go; at which they reproved her, reminding her that no one is necessary anywhere; the gap would be well taken care of, they knew. And then they sang a hymn.

Then through the hymn came another sound like the pain of a million broken hearts wrung out in one full drop, one sob. And a horror of great darkness was upon me, for I knew what it was—the Cry of the Blood.

Then thundered a voice, the Voice of the Lord: "And He said, What hast thou done? The voice of thy brothers' blood crieth unto Me from the ground."

The tom-toms still beat heavily, the darkness still shuddered and shivered about me; I heard the yells of the devil-dancers and the weird wild shriek of the devil-possessed just outside the gate.

What does it matter, after all? It has gone on for years; it will go on for years. Why make such a fuss about it?

God forgive us! God arouse us! Shame us out of our callousness! Shame us out of our sin!

•   •   •

After I had finished reading, I sent another letter to Holland: "Forget what I wrote in my last letter; I hope to die in harness."

•   •   •

Has God told you something as you have read this book? If you heard Him, do not delay your obedience. Act now. Do not wait until it is too late. If you need help on your way into, or within, the Palace of Plenty, contact a mature Christian in your neighborhood. He will tell you, "Jesus is the door!"

By Corrie ten Boom

Amazing Love
Common Sense Not Needed
Defeated Enemies
Not Good If Detached
Marching Orders for the End Battle
Plenty for Everyone
A Prisoner and Yet . . .

The Hiding Place
By Corrie ten Boom with John and Elizabeth Sherrill

Tramp for the Lord
By Corrie ten Boom with Jamie Buckingham

This book was produced by CLC Publications. We hope it has been life-changing and has given you a fresh experience of God through the work of the Holy Spirit. CLC Publications is an outreach of CLC Ministries International, a global literature mission with work in over 50 countries. If you would like to know more about us or are interested in opportunities to serve with a faith mission, we invite you to contact us at:

CLC Ministries International
PO Box 1449
Fort Washington, PA 19034

Phone: (215) 542-1242
E-mail: mail@clcusa.org
Website: www.clcusa.org

- -

DO YOU LOVE GOOD CHRISTIAN BOOKS?
Do you have a heart for worldwide missions?

You can receive a FREE subscription to
CLC's newsletter on global literature missions
Order by e-mail at:
clcheartbeat@clcusa.org
or fill in the coupon below and mail to:
P.O. Box 1449
Fort Washington, PA 19034

FREE *HEARTBEAT* SUBSCRIPTION!

Name: _____

Address: _____

_____

Phone: _____ E-mail: _____